NOËL
COWARD

IN HIS OWN WORDS

NOËL COWARD

IN HIS OWN WORDS

⁙ ⁙ ⁙

Compiled and introduced by
Barry Day

Methuen

Published by Methuen 2004

1 3 5 7 9 10 8 6 4 2

Original version (entitled *Noël Coward: A Life in Quotes*) first
published in Great Britain in 1999 by Metro Books (an imprint of
Metro Publishing Limited)

This revised and enlarged version published by
Methuen Publishing Limited
215 Vauxhall Bridge Road
London SW1V 1EJ
www.methuen.co.uk

Methuen Publishing Limited Reg. No. 3543167

ISBN 0 413 77441 4

A CIP catalogue for this title is available from the British Library.

Typeset by SX Composing DTP, Rayleigh, Essex

Printed and bound in Great Britain
by Mackays of Chatham plc, Chatham, Kent

How invaluable it would be . . . if just once, for a brief spell, I could see myself clearly from the outside, as others saw me. How helpful it would be, moving so continually across the public vision, to know what that vision really observed, to note objectively what it was in my personality that moved some people to like and applaud me and aroused in others such irritation and resentment. How salutary it would be to watch the whole performance through from the front of the house, to see to what extent the mannerisms were effective and note when and where they should be cut down.

Future Indefinite (1954)

Quotes *on* Coward

The Congreve of our time.

Arnold Bennett

Destiny's tot.

Alexander Woollcott

A sort of Marconi of the artistic world.

Ruby Miller (Mrs Max Darewski)

He is simply a phenomenon and one that is unlikely to occur ever again in theatre history – actor, director, dramatist unrivalled this century.

Terence Rattigan

. . . he was a master because he so bravely and brilliantly made use of the sentimental as well as the comic and because under that clipped precision, there was tenderness, particularly towards the unimportant, the bit parts and the failures.

Sir John Betjeman at the thanksgiving service (1973)

(He is) his own invention and contribution to the twentieth century.

John Osborne

There are probably greater painters than Noël, greater novelists than Noël, greater librettists, greater composers of music, greater singers, greater dancers, greater comedians, greater tragedians, greater stage producers, greater film directors, greater cabaret artists, greater TV stars. If there are, they are fourteen different people. Only one man combined all fourteen different labels – The Master.

Lord Louis Mountbatten at Noël's 70th birthday party (1969)

Even the youngest of us will know, in fifty years' time, precisely what is meant by 'a very Noël Coward sort of person'.

Kenneth Tynan

CONTENTS

⁙ ⁙ ⁙

INTRODUCTION

The Word According to Coward

⋮⋮⋮   ⋮⋮⋮   ⋮⋮⋮

Did Noël Coward use the words – or did the words use him?

Certainly, you'd be hard put to name anyone in the twentieth century who employed the English language with the same precision, concision and consistency as he did. And his range was remarkable. In the dialogue of his plays, in verse, song lyrics, essays, stories, letters, auto-biography, interviews – and perhaps most particularly in private conversation – words were his weapons, and 'wordsmith' both his occupation and his preoccupation.

An essentially private person for so public a persona, he consistently used the words to create an image behind which he could hide his more vulnerable emotions. So effective was this defence mechanism that Coward has rarely been given the credit for even possessing ordinary sensibilities – although he provided a clue to the contrary in one of his plays. In *Shadow Play* he has Gertrude Lawrence say: 'Small talk, a lot of small talk with other thoughts going on behind.' The small talk and the apparent frivolity are what we employ when to say what we really *mean* would prove too painful.

American novelist Peter de Vries once skewered one of his own characters by saying that 'on the surface he was deep – but deep down he was shallow'. Precisely the opposite was true of Noël Coward but, ironically, it was largely the posthumous publication of his *Diaries* and a study of his private papers that provided the portrait with its present light and shade.

Coward was a curious man – in the strict sense of that word. He was fascinated by the people with whom he shared the planet, by the feelings they apparently had in common and the behaviour – particularly the patterns of speech – that differentiated them, so that the same words from different speakers could convey quite different meanings. And everything he saw and heard he recorded.

One speech in *Present Laughter* (1939) will serve as an example. The actor Garry Essendine is making stilted small talk with the aspiring young playwright Roland Maule:

> GARRY: You've come all the way from Uckfield?
> ROLAND: It isn't very far.
> GARRY: Well, it sort of *sounds* far, doesn't it?
> ROLAND: (*defensively*) It's quite near Lewes.
> GARRY: Then there's nothing to worry about, is there?

A sociological thesis couldn't define the two characters more precisely.

Coward is generally considered a man who lived in and for the moment. In fact, he never forgot a humble past and constantly recreated it in his depiction (often more nostalgically affectionate than realistic) of working-class life. He was also concerned – increasingly so as the years went by – with the purpose of life. Among the earliest musings he privately committed to youthful paper, he debates with himself the value of religion. In public, the instinctive barrier of words is erected.

Did he believe in God?, David Frost once asked him in

a television interview. 'We've never been intimate – but maybe we do have a few things in common,' Noël replied, lighting the ever-present cigarette and disappearing behind a cloud of smoke.

In a later interview he was asked for the one valedictory word he felt would sum up the play that had been his life. He bought himself a little time by pondering aloud the risk of sounding corny before settling on: 'LOVE . . . To know that you are among people whom you love and who love you. That has made all the successes wonderful – much more wonderful than they'd have been anyway. And I don't think there's anything more to be said after that.'

Seen in this light, Coward's use of words is significantly different from that of the two writers with whom he is most often compared. A Wilde epigram may have a greater surface shine, but drop it and all you are left with are fragments. Pick up one by Shaw and you may well cut yourself, for it lacks kindness. Coward is altogether more comfortable company because his is the language of the good conversationalist and the kind man; his *bons mots* deal with the stuff of all our lives, and perhaps what defines him most is that you feel you have thought these thoughts and might have expressed many of them yourself – if only the words had fallen in the right order.

In this collection I have naturally included many of the 'classic' Coward lines but I have also delved into the private papers and unpublished material for lines that – even out of context – show a mind in the making and the emergence of themes he would reorchestrate and refine as the years went by. Where possible I have attributed the quotations to their specific context but inevitably – as with all the great wits – some have become part of the legend by word of mouth. Coward himself summed up the dilemma best when he declared: 'I'm naturally a witty man. I have been and doubtless I always shall be. In my time I've said some noteworthy and exceptionally memorable things. If the remarks with which I am credited – and never made – are really good, I acknowledge them. I generally work myself into the belief that I originally said them.'

This collection reveals more than merely a unique wit – the precious commodity he always felt should be 'a glorious treat like caviar', not 'spread about like marmalade'. It depicts a man of depth, compassion and London pride. After the 'cocktails and laughter' there was infinitely more than just 'a talent to amuse'.

Barry Day
2004

PART ONE

⣿ ⣿ ⣿

'Why Must the Show Go On?'

To Coward, the theatre was virtually a religion, a 'temple of illusion', and he could not bear to see that temple desecrated by philistines, either from within or from without. Typically, his punishment was ridicule.

Genuine lack of talent always appalled him, as did some of the theatre's more arcane traditions. After half a century of watching gallant 'troupers', young or old, dragging themselves through their 'Laugh, Clown, Laugh' routines to ensure that the show went on regardless, he decided he had finally had enough and, in a song in his Café de Paris cabaret act in the early 1950s, he posed the question no one was meant to ask:

> *Why must the show go on?*
> *It can't be all that indispensable,*
> *To me it really isn't sensible*
> *On the whole*
> *To play a leading role*
> *While fighting those tears you can't control,*
> *Why kick up your legs*
> *When draining the dregs*
> *Of sorrow's bitter cup?*
> *Because you have read*
> *Some idiot has said*
> *'The Curtain must go up!'*
>
> 'Why Must the Show Go On?' (1954)

Not that his own career ran entirely smoothly:

I partnered a girl named Eileen Dennis, and we were engaged by the Elysée Restaurant (now the Café de Paris) to appear during dinner and supper.

A slow waltz, a tango, and a rather untidy one-step made up our programme. Later, owing to popular demand (from Eileen Dennis's mother), we introduced a *pierrot fantasia* for which we changed into cherry-coloured sateen and tulle ruffs. No South African millionaires threw diamond sunbursts at Eileen's feet. We were neither of us ever invited to appear naked out of pies at private supper parties, in fact the whole engagement from the point of view of worldly experience was decidedly disappointing.

Present Indicative (1937)

MR. NOËL COWARD MAKING MENTAL NOTES FOR THE FIRST PART OF "CAVALCADE."

His début came at a ridiculously early age and he would look back on his younger self with awed objectivity:

> I was a brazen, odious little prodigy, over-pleased
> with myself and precocious to a degree.
>
> *Present Indicative* (1937)

⁙ ⁙ ⁙

> Miss Joan Carroll and Mr. Noël Coward as the
> Toadstool and the Mushroom headed delightfully a
> little troupe of various small and engaging fungi.
>
> *The Times* reviewing *An Autumn Idyll* (1912)

Reflecting on an early performance:

> I am certain that, could my adult self have been
> present . . . he would have crept out, at the first coy
> gurgle, and been mercifully sick outside.
>
> *Present Indicative* (1937)

⁙ ⁙ ⁙

> *An infant prodigy of nine*
> *Is shoved upon the stage in white.*
> *She starts off in a dismal whine*
> *About a Dark and Stormy night,*
> *A burglar whose heart is true,*
> *Despite his wicked looking face!*
> *And what a little child can do*
> *To save her Mama's jewel case!*
>
> *Concert Types* (1917)

⁙ ⁙ ⁙

I was a talented child, God knows, and when washed
and smarmed down a bit, passably attractive; but I
was, I believe, one of the worst boy actors ever
inflicted on the paying public.

Present Indicative (1937)

⁜   ⁜   ⁜

It really is unbelievably difficult to act like a moron
when one isn't a moron.

To a child actor colleague, Michael Mac Liammoir

⁜   ⁜   ⁜

PERRY: I love *Peter Pan*.
ZELDA: That's because you've got a mother-fixation.
   All sensitive lads with mother-fixations worship
   Peter Pan.

Waiting in the Wings (1960)

And if it wasn't Peter, it was that other Pan fellow. He was introduced by his
childhood friend, Esmé Wynne . . .

She wrote poems. Reams and reams of them, love
songs, sonnets, and villanelles: alive with elves,
mermaids, leafy glades, and Pan (a good deal of Pan).

Present Indicative (1937)

Which duly led Noël to try his hand at a novel to be called *Cherry Pan* . . .

Cherry Pan, I regret to tell you, was the daughter of
the Great God Pan and was garrulous and tiresome
to the point of nausea. Having materialised suddenly
on a summer evening in Sussex, she proceeded with

excruciating pagan archness to wreak havoc in a
country parsonage before returning winsomely to her
woodland glades and elfin grots. I remember being
bitterly offended by a friend who suggested that the
title should be changed to *Bedpan*.

Speech at a literary lunch

⁑   ⁑   ⁑

There was a loveable old professor who suddenly
inherited a family of merry little kiddos . . . We were
all jolly and mischievous in act one and then we all
went to sleep in a magic garden and became elves and
gnomes and what have you for acts two and three.
Some of us have remained fairies to this day.

George Banks in 'Me and the Girls'

As a child actor himself under the eagle eye of a 'stage mother' he had
plenty of opportunity to study the phenomenon at close quarters as audition
succeeded audition:

> *Don't put your daughter on the stage, Mrs. Worthington,*
> *Don't put your daughter on the stage,*
> *The profession is overcrowded*
> *And the struggle's pretty tough*
> *And admitting the fact*
> *She's burning to act*
> *That isn't quite enough.*

'Mrs. Worthington' (1936)

It was rarely a pretty sight and the song was his attempt to provide a corrective:

It is a genuine *cri de coeur* . . . Unhappily, its
effectiveness, from the point of view of propaganda,

has been negligible. I had hoped, by writing it, to discourage misguided maternal ambition, to deter those dreadful eager mothers from making beasts of themselves, boring the hell out of me and wasting their own and my time, but I have not succeeded . . . ninety-nine out of a hundred of the letters they write to me refer to it with roguish indulgence, obviously secure in the conviction that it could not in any circumstance apply to them. This is saddening, of course, but realising that the road of the social reformer is paved with disillusions I have determined to rise above it.

The Noël Coward Song Book (1953)

On seeing one of these child prodigies dominate and sink a play, despite considerable critical acclaim, Coward remarked as he left the theatre:

Two things in that play should have been cut. The second act and that child's throat.

Attributed

On another occasion he was less than pleased with a child actor's performance in a musical version of *Gone With the Wind*. When an on-stage horse performed a natural function – perhaps in a spirit of constructive criticism – Coward observed:

If they'd stuffed the child's head up the horse's arse, they would have solved two problems at once.

His views on what constituted good theatre were deeply held and unchanged throughout his life. Nor did he miss many opportunities to restate them:

The theatre must be treated with respect. It is a house of strange enchantment, a temple of dreams.

⠿   ⠿   ⠿

What is most emphatically is *not* and never will be is
a scruffy, illiterate, fumed-oak drill-hall serving as a
temporary soap-box for political propaganda.

'A Warning to Actors', *Sunday Times* (1961)

⠿   ⠿   ⠿

Consider the public. Treat it with tact and courtesy.
It will accept much from you if you are clever enough
to win it to your side. Never fear it or despise it. Coax
it, charm it, interest it, stimulate it, shock it now and
then if you must, make it laugh, make it cry and make
it think, but above all . . . never, never, never bore
the living hell out of it.

Sunday Times (1961)

⠿   ⠿   ⠿

. . . as long as I continue to write plays to be acted in
theatres, I shall strain every fibre to see that they are
clear, well constructed and strong enough in content,
either serious or funny, to keep an average paying
audience interested from 8:30 until 11:15. Here
endeth the first and last and, for me, only lesson.

Diaries (1956)

American producer, Gilbert Miller was Noël's own first mentor on the
subject of what constituted a good play . . .

He said that someone had told his father (Henry
Miller), who in turn had told him, that the construction
of a play was as important as the foundations of a

house, whereas dialogue, however good, could only, at best, be considered as interior decoration.

Present Indicative (1937)

Noël took the advice so much to heart that in later years he would preach it to others . . .

Before the first word of the first act is written, the last act should be clearly in the author's mind, if not actually written out in the form of a synopsis. Dialogue, for those who have a talent for it, is easy; but construction, with or without talent, is difficult and is of paramount importance. I know this sounds like heresy in this era of highly-praised, half-formulated moods, but no mood, however exquisite, is likely to hold the attention of an audience for two hours and a half unless it is based on a solid structure.

Future Indefinite (1954)

⠿　⠿　⠿

ROLAND: Plots aren't important, it's ideas that matter. Look at Chekhov.
GARRY: In addition to ideas I think we might concede Chekhov a certain flimsy sense of psychology, don't you?

Present Laughter (1939)

⠿　⠿　⠿

The most important ingredients of a play are life, death, food, sex and money – but not necessarily in that order.

Dick Richards, *The Wit of Noël Coward* (1968)

⁜   ⁜   ⁜

Your characters should say less at one go, unless it is
a highly dramatic scene. *Don't* under rate your
Audience so dreadfully – instead of letting your
people *say* how and what they're feeling – let them
express it more subtly – the Audience will get it all
right.

Advice to his literary soulmate, Esmé Wynne (c. 1915)

And a pre-emptive word of warning to the current crop of gay young
directors who insist on preaching the flawed gospel of what 'darling
Noël *would* have done or written, if it hadn't been for that stupid
censorship . . .'

Suggestion is always more interesting than statement.

⁜   ⁜   ⁜

HELEN: The great thing in this world is not to be
obvious – over *anything*!

The Vortex (1924)

Despite his many talents, writing plays was what he did first and last and
what he always came back to. It was his work:

The only way to enjoy life is to work. Work is much
more fun than fun.

Observer Sayings of the Week (1963)

⁜   ⁜   ⁜

· 11 ·

It seems to me that a professional writer should be animated by no other motive than the desire to write and, by doing so, to earn his living.

Introduction to *Play Parade* (1934)

On the nature of inspiration . . .

Ideas do not come to you through wandering around in the woods, hoping for inspiration. It just isn't there. It's in your head.

⁙ ⁙ ⁙

She felt suddenly cheerful, with that cheerfulness only writers know when they have successfully completed a morning's work.

'Bon Voyage'

⁙ ⁙ ⁙

I can see no particular virtue in writing quickly; on the contrary, I am well aware that too great a facility is often dangerous and should be curbed when it shows signs of getting the bit too firmly between its teeth. No reputable writer should permit his talent to bolt with him.

Future Indefinite (1954)

In 1956 in Jamaica he took up and took to writing verse . . .

I find it quite fascinating to write at random, sometimes in rhyme, sometimes not. I am trying to discipline myself away from too much discipline, by which I mean that my experience and training in

lyric writing has made me inclined to stick too closely
to a rigid form. It is strange that technical accuracy
should occasionally banish magic, but it does. The
carefully rhymed verses, which I find it very difficult
not to do, are, on the whole, less effective and
certainly less moving than the free ones.

Diaries (1956)

Even though anyone charged with typing what he wrote had quite a task . . .

My handwriting looks as though Chinese ants have
crawled all over the paper.

To Cole Lesley – *Remembered Laughter* (1976)

⁂   ⁂   ⁂

I have a slight reforming urge, but I have rather
cunningly kept it down.

The Times (1969)

⁂   ⁂   ⁂

GARRY: If you wish to be a playwright . . . go and
get yourself a job as a butler in a repertory
company, if they'll have you. Learn from the
ground up how plays are constructed and what is
actable and what isn't. Then sit down and write at
least twenty plays one after the other, and if you
can manage to get the twenty-first produced for a
Sunday night performance you'll be damned
lucky.

Present Laughter (1939)

Nonetheless, it was a *skill* that one honed in the live theatre, not the study:

> It's no use to go and take courses in playwriting any more than it's much use taking courses in acting. Better play to a bad matinée in Hull, it will teach you much more than a year of careful instruction.
>
> Television interview (1969)

In the same interview he would add:

> Come to think of it, I never did play to a *good* matinée in Hull . . .

His own start had been far from stellar. On his first visit to New York in 1921 he found no one beating a path to his rented door. Finally he was offered a fee of $500 by *Metropolitan Magazine* to adapt *I'll Leave It To You* into a short story:

> I reflected gleefully that for $500 I would gladly consider turning *War and Peace* into a music-hall sketch.
>
> *Present Indicative* (1937)

☷ ☷ ☷

> Young playwrights would do well to compare their reviews with their royalty statements.
>
> Dick Richards, *The Wit of Noël Coward* (1968)

During his own period of dramatic apprenticeship Noël was in the habit of jotting down scraps of dialogue that might come in useful later on:

> She was so *embonpoint* before her marriage that her fiancé used to use her as a cake stand.

⁘   ⁘   ⁘

She fell down a lift shaft on Ascension Day – so perverse of her.

⁘   ⁘   ⁘

– As Oscar Wilde might have said, golf is essentially the massive in pursuit of the minute.
– I don't see why you should imagine the poor man would ever say anything so unfunny.

⁘   ⁘   ⁘

Sarcasm from you is reminiscent of a bevy of elephants leaping round a gadfly and imagining they're teasing it.

⁘   ⁘   ⁘

She's the kind of woman who only uses the Bible for blasphemous reference.

⁘   ⁘   ⁘

– Do you think a doctor would give a professional secret away?
– Of course not – honour among thieves.

⁘   ⁘   ⁘

Never take anything seriously, except perhaps bath salts.

⠿ ⠿ ⠿

My dear, there's nothing so ordinary as to try to be extraordinary.

⠿ ⠿ ⠿

She didn't like mustard, otherwise she was perfectly normal.

⠿ ⠿ ⠿

It was just that she had a complete set of Ella Wheeler Wilcox that prejudiced you.

⠿ ⠿ ⠿

My dear, she just missed being beautiful by buying her clothes ready-made.

⠿ ⠿ ⠿

She lives at Croydon and wants to see more of life.

From an early stage he was associated with the writing of comedies:

To me the essence of good comedy writing is that perfectly ordinary phrases such as 'Just fancy!' should, by virtue of their context, achieve greater laughs than the most literate epigrams. Some of the biggest laughs in *Hay Fever* occur on such lines as 'Go on', 'No, there isn't, is there?' and 'This haddock's disgusting'. There are many other glittering examples of my sophistication in the same vein.

Comedy is nearly always despised in its generation
and honoured more latterly – except by the public.

Dick Richards, *The Wit of Noël Coward* (1968)

He enjoyed humour that relied on the substitution of another word – often the opposite – for the original . . .

Let me be the eighth to congratulate you.

⁜ ⁜ ⁜

Poor man . . . he's completely unspoilt by failure.

⁜ ⁜ ⁜

He was an abstract painter with a very abstract talent.

⁜ ⁜ ⁜

There is less in this than meets the eye.

⁜ ⁜ ⁜

His thinking is the triumph of never mind over doesn't matter.

⁜ ⁜ ⁜

She suffered for years in a lack of concentration camp.

⁜ ⁜ ⁜

– It will bring out the colour in your eyes.
– Much better leave it where it is, then.

Cole Lesley – *Remembered Laughter* (1976)

Or the use of the ordinary in an unexpected context . . .

> RUTH: The mousse wasn't quite right.
> CHARLES: It *looked* a bit hysterical but it tasted delicious.

Blithe Spirit (1941)

When asked to admire one of Romney Marsh's dramatic sunsets . . .

> Too red. Very affected.

(To be fair, Oscar Wilde had said something very similar.)

⁙ ⁙ ⁙

> LESTER: Louise was always an angel but her hats were misguided.

Long Island Sound (1947)

⁙ ⁙ ⁙

> . . . her loveliness triumphed over many inopportune bows and ostrich feathers.

Describing Laurette Taylor in *Present Indicative* (1937)

⁙ ⁙ ⁙

> She was wearing a hat that looked like it was in a great hurry and couldn't stay around for long.

Tonight At 8:30 (1935)

⁙ ⁙ ⁙

His eyes looked as though they were permanently scared of being separated from one another and seemed to be edging closer and closer together.

'Mrs. Capper's Birthday'

Her enormous bouffant hairdo diminished her sharp little face so that she resembled a marmoset wearing a busby.

'Mrs. Capper's Birthday'

⁑　　⁑　　⁑

She has no go in her, that girl. She borrowed the top of my Thermos, and never returned it. Shallow, very shallow.

The Young Idea (1922)

⁑　　⁑　　⁑

PAWNIE: Look at the furniture . . . look at that lamp-shade! . . . Too unrestrained. Such a bad example to the servants.

The Vortex (1924)

⁑　　⁑　　⁑

My dear, always make sure your eyebrows are properly lit. You can't play comedy without eyebrows.

To actress Patience Collier

⁑　　⁑　　⁑

It's so easy to get laughs and so difficult to control them. And that's the essence of comedy.

BBC Television interview, 'Great Acting' (1966)

⁚⁚⁚   ⁚⁚⁚   ⁚⁚⁚

CRESTWELL: Comedies of manners swiftly become obsolete when there are no longer any manners.

Relative Values (1951)

But with him the play was – first, last and always – the thing . . .

I am light-minded. I would inevitably write a comedy if – God help me! – I wanted to write a play with a message.

Diaries (1959)

Coward had no time for artistic pretension in the theatre and frequently observed that the avant-garde piece hailed by the intellectual press often failed to find comparable acclaim at the box office. This was not the route he ever intended to pursue:

I've never written for the intelligentsia. Sixteen curtain calls and closed on Saturday.

Interview with the *Daily Mirror*

⁚⁚⁚   ⁚⁚⁚   ⁚⁚⁚

My plays are written for the public and not for that small galaxy of scruffy critics and pretentious savants who know little and do less.

Diaries (1956)

⠿   ⠿   ⠿

I am quite prepared to admit that during my fifty-odd years of theatre-going, I have on many occasions been profoundly moved by plays about the Common Man, as in my fifty-odd years of restaurant-going I have frequently enjoyed tripe and onions, but I am not prepared to admit that an exclusive diet of either would be completely satisfying.

The Common Man, unless written or portrayed with genius, is not dramatically nearly so interesting as he is claimed to be.

'A Warning to Actors', *Sunday Times* (1961)

⠿   ⠿   ⠿

The age of the Common Man has taken over a nation which owes its very existence to uncommon men.

Diaries (1956)

⠿   ⠿   ⠿

I am becoming almighty sick of the Welfare State; sick of general 'commonness', sick of ugly voices, sick of bad manners and teenagers and debased values.

Diaries (1963)

⠿   ⠿   ⠿

It is dull to write incessantly about tramps and prostitutes as it is to write incessantly about dukes and duchesses and even suburban maters and paters, and it is bigoted and stupid to believe that tramps and prostitutes and under-privileged housewives frying onions and using ironing boards are automatically the salt of the earth and that nobody else is worth bothering about. It is true that a writer should try to hold the mirror up to nature, although there are aspects of nature that would be better unreflected.

'A Warning to Pioneers', *Sunday Times* (1961)

On the other hand, the answer was not to go to the opposite extreme of mindless froth:

I would like to prove that talent and material count for more than sequins and tits.

Referring to *Ace of Clubs* in his *Diaries* (1950)

Often the hardest part of a show was deciding what to call it. When producers Charles Russell and Lance Hamilton were looking for a name for the first of the *Night of 100 Stars* charity galas, there was a suggestion that it might be called *Summer Stars* – to which Noël quipped: 'Some are not!' On another occasion the author of a new show was debating what to call it and suggested *An Enquiry into Certain Aspects of the Dogmas of World War One* – to which Coward replied: 'Too snappy.' And when Russian-born Vernon Duke (*né* Vladimir Dukelsky) produced his first musical, *Yvonne,* Noël retitled it: *Ivan the Terrible.*

When there was some difficulty in deciding on a title for the first Coward anthology show, one of the production team suggested *Cream of Coward.* 'That would be asking for trouble,' Noël replied bleakly. Nevertheless, he orchestrated the dairy theme. At his suggestion the show was eventually called *Cowardy Custard* (1972).

And when it came to performing the plays:

I think the most dangerous theory advanced in modern days is that you have to feel what you do for eight performances a week. It's out of the question. And also, acting is not a state of being. Acting is acting . . . It's giving an impression of feeling. If it's real feeling, then you're very liable to lose your performance and lose the attention of the audience, because if you lose yourself, you're liable to lose them.

BBC Television interview, 'Great Acting' (1966)

⁙⁙⁙ ⁙⁙⁙ ⁙⁙⁙

Timing is 70% of acting.

Attributed

⁙⁙⁙ ⁙⁙⁙ ⁙⁙⁙

Writing is more important than acting, for one very good reason: it lasts. Stage acting only lives in people's memories as long as they live. Writing is creative; acting is interpretive. Only occasionally does very good acting become creative.

Sunday Telegraph (1966)

Coward was that unusual phenomenon – a playwright who also acted.

Acting is an instinct. A gift that is often given to people who are very silly as people. But as they come on to the stage, up goes the temperature.

⁙⁙⁙ ⁙⁙⁙ ⁙⁙⁙

I don't know what it [star quality] is, but I've got it.

Kathleen Tynan, *The Life of Kenneth Tynan* (1987)

Later – in his 1967 play of that name – he would attempt to define it . . .

DIRECTOR: . . . I leave to the last the question of talent. That's the pay-off, the definitive answer to all the silly riddles. That's their basic power, their natural gift for acting. I don't suppose a star has ever acted really badly in her life. I don't believe she could if she tried. That is her one reality, the foundation upon which the whole structure of her charm and personality rests, and, believe you me, it's rock solid. But that Star Quality is what transcends everything else. It's beyond definition and beyond praise. Whether they're born with it or how and where they manage to acquire it, I neither know nor care, but it's there all right. It's there as strongly in comedy as it is in tragedy.

You can be at a matinée in Manchester – or even in Hull. The play is lousy, the fortnight's notice is up on the board and the audience is so dull, you think half of them must be dead. That was the first act.

By the last they're sitting on the edge of their seats and at the final curtain they scream the place down. The hair rises on your scalp, the tears are cascading down your face and you solemnly bless the day that you were born.

And *that*, my friends, is Star Quality.

Much as he adored the craft of acting, he had few illusions about some of its practitioners:

> Theatrical people are notoriously facile of emotion, and frequently victimised by their own foolish sentimentality.
>
> *Present Indicative* (1937)

⁂ ⁂ ⁂

> BRIAN (THE AUTHOR): Why can't people in the theatre behave like normal human beings?
> TONY (DIRECTOR'S ASSISTANT): There wouldn't be a theatre if they did.
>
> *Star Quality* (1967)

⁂ ⁂ ⁂

> All acting worth the name is ham. We rehearse for weeks to hide it, but it's there all the time.
>
> To Marie Tempest (1934)

Advising a young actress on the need to project:

> When young I remember having a downward-looking view from the Gallery of Tree and Hawtrey and I could hear every word. But now, swathed in stardom in the stalls, I find I don't hear as well as in the old days.
>
> Dick Richards, *The Wit of Noël Coward* (1968)

⁂ ⁂ ⁂

> The actor is a recollection with a lot of gold dust on it.

Advice to his fellow actors:

> Speak clearly, don't bump into people, and if you
> must have motivation, think of your pay packet on
> Friday.
>
> Speech to the Gallery First Nighters' Club (1962)

And on the subject of stage fright . . .

> It is only natural, I think, that established stars
> should become more and more prone to stage fright
> as the years stack up behind them . . . I have little
> patience, however, with those who indulge their
> nervousness to the extent of spoiling their
> performances . . . If an actor is undisciplined enough
> to allow his own self-consciousness to intervene
> between himself and his talent, he should leave the
> theatrical profession and devote himself to some less
> agitating profession.
>
> *Past Conditional* (1965)

In *Sigh No More* (1945) an enthusiastic but inexperienced young male dancer playing Harlequin had forgotten to wear his 'protector'. When he had leapt about a little, Noël instructed the choreographer, Wendy Toye:

> For God's sake, go and tell that young man to take
> that Rockingham tea service out of his tights.

:::   :::   :::

> LORRAINE (THE STAR): God preserve us from
> enthusiastic amateurs who have ghastly theories
> about acting and keep on talking about rhythm and
> colour.

BRYAN: I thought his *Hamlet* was marvellous.
LORRAINE: All that unbleached linen and kapok.
The Closet scene looked like a tea-tent.

Star Quality (1967)

⦙⦙⦙   ⦙⦙⦙   ⦙⦙⦙

JOANNA: I expect it's because you're an actor,
they're always apt to be a bit *papier mâché*.
GARRY: Just puppets, Joanna dear, creatures of
tinsel and sawdust, how clever of you to have
noticed it.

Present Laughter (1939)

⦙⦙⦙   ⦙⦙⦙   ⦙⦙⦙

Actors are incredibly silly, and leading ladies idiotic.

Diaries (1961)

Noël's put-downs of leading ladies were legendary. In the 1964 revival of *Hay Fever* when Edith Evans consistently read the line, 'You can see Marlow on a clear day, so they tell me' as '. . . on a *very* clear day', Noël corrected her with, 'No, dear, on a *very* clear day you can see Marlowe *and* Beaumont *and* Fletcher.' At a later performance she 'took her curtain calls as though she had just been un-nailed from the cross'.

In the 1956 television version of *Blithe Spirit*, Claudette Colbert ('I'd wring her neck – if I could find it') was fluffing her lines badly:

– Oh, dear, I knew them backwards this morning.
– And that's just the way you're delivering them, dear.

Judy Campbell was on a wartime tour of the provinces with Coward. Exasperated with what she considered his temperamental behaviour, she finally snapped:

> – Oh, I could just *throw* something at you!
> – Try starting with my lines.

(1943)

On Gladys Cooper's inability to remember hers in *Relative Values* (1951):

> I did not expect word perfection at the first rehearsal but I had rather hoped for it on the first night.

To an actress whose first-night performance was plagued with technical problems:

> You managed to play the first act of my little comedy tonight with all the Chinese flair and light-hearted brilliance of Lady Macbeth.

Having seen the French actress Simone Signoret play Lady Macbeth in English for the first time, he summed up the production as:

> *Aimez-vous Glamis?*

Washington Post (1969)

When an actress playing Queen Victoria had left Coward distinctly unamused:

> I never realised before that Albert married beneath his station.

Evening Standard (1965)

⁙　⁙　⁙

She stopped the show – but then the show wasn't
really travelling very fast.

⁜   ⁜   ⁜

MAUD: I was in *Miss Mouse* at the Adelphi and I had
   a number in the last act called 'Don't Play the Fool
   with a Schoolgirl'. It used to stop the show.
CORA: So far as I can remember it was the notices
   that stopped the show.

Waiting in the Wings (1961)

Coward once attended a session of the Actors' Studio and heard Lee
Strasberg recall Eleanor Duse:

{He} explained that when she smiled she didn't
merely smile with her mouth, but with every part of
her body! Which comes under the heading of the
neatest trick of the week.

Diaries (1965)

But even the most eminent of theatrical *eminences grises* has to start
somewhere . . .

DAME ROSIE:
My very first step
Was Shakespearean 'rep'
Where an awful old 'Ham' used to train us.
I'd nothing to do
In The Dream *and* The Shrew
But I carried a spear
In King John *and* King Lear
And a hatchet in Coriolanus.
I ranted for years

In pavilions on piers
Til my spirits were really at zero,
Then I got a small role
Of a Tart with a soul
In a play by Sir Arthur Pinero.

'Three Theatrical Dames' from *Hoi Polloi* (1947)
– unproduced musical

⁙　　⁙　　⁙

Many years ago I remember a famous actress
explaining to me with perfect seriousness that before
making an entrance she always stood aside and let God
go on first. I can also remember that on that particular
occasion He gave a singularly uninspired performance.

Stage Fright (1965)

⁙　　⁙　　⁙

When I eventually write my book on the theatre
there will be a whole chapter devoted to leading
ladies' dresses and hair. They are invariably the main
stumbling-blocks. Leading ladies' husbands may also
come in for some acrid comment.

Diaries (1961)

⁙　　⁙　　⁙

Poor darling glamorous stars everywhere, their lives
are so lonely and wretched and frustrated. Nothing
but applause, flowers, Rolls-Royces, expensive hotel
suites, constant adulation. It's too pathetic and
wrings the heart.

Diaries (1955)

⠿   ⠿   ⠿

Great big glamorous stars can be very tiresome.

Diaries (1956)

⠿   ⠿   ⠿

It is sad to think how many of our glamorous leading ladies are round the bend.

Diaries (1958)

⠿   ⠿   ⠿

She got in a rage
About age
And retired, in a huff, from the stage.
Which, taken all round, was a pity
Because she was still fairly pretty
But she got in a rage
About age . . .

And she moaned and she wept and she wailed
And she roared and she ranted and railed
And retired, very heavily veiled,
From the stage.

'Epitaph for an Elderly Actress', *Collected Verse* (1984)

⠿   ⠿   ⠿

God preserve me in future from female stars. I don't suppose He will. I really am too old and tired to go through all these tired old hoops.

Diaries (1956)

But without a doubt his *leading* leading lady – both professionally and personally – was Gertrud Alexandra Dagmar Lawrence-Klausen (Gertie Lawrence). They met as fellow child actors in 1913 and Coward recorded their meeting in *Present Indicative*. She was, he recalled:

> A vivacious child with ringlets to whom I took an instant fancy . . . her face was far from pretty, but tremendously alive. She was very *mondaine,* carried a handbag with a powder-puff and frequently dabbed her generously turned-up nose. She confided to me that her name was Gertrude Lawrence, but that I was to call her Gert because everybody did.

Although the names 'Noël and Gertie' became indissolubly linked, in fact they only appeared together twice as adult actors – in *Private Lives* (1930) and *Tonight At 8:30* (1936). So popular were they with the public that they talked often of the future plays he would write for the two of them. Their relationship was based on their irreverent affection for each other. Even the

humble telegram could be turned into a medium for wit when she was the subject. On opening in her first straight play:

> LEGITIMATE AT LAST STOP WON'T
> MOTHER BE PLEASED

On a subsequent first night:

> A WARM HAND ON YOUR OPENING

And on her 1940 marriage to Richard Aldrich:

> DEAR MRS. A HOORAY HOORAY
> AT LAST YOU ARE DEFLOWERED
> ON THIS AS EVERY OTHER DAY
> I LOVE YOU NOEL COWARD

On one occasion Coward was invited to write a typical Hollywood film script to star Gertie. He replied:

> REGRET CANNOT WRITE LIFE OF SARAH
> BERNHARDT FOR GERTRUDE LAWRENCE
> STOP TOO BUSY WRITING LIFE OF
> ELEONORA DUSE FOR BEATRICE LILLIE

(Or in some versions – 'St Teresa for Mae West')

But even affection was not allowed to stand in the way of professional perfectionism. Miss Lawrence was known to sing famously flat on occasion . . .

> If you would sing a little *more* out of tune, darling,
> you would find yourself singing in thirds, which
> would be a *great* improvement.
>
> *Noël Coward Song Book* (1953)

Coward was as objective about his own stage persona as he was about other people's. Asked in a television interview if he had ever been the subject of a 'put-down', he replied:

> Yes, I once left a stage door and there was a glamorous crowd welcoming me with autograph books, which I was graciously signing, when I heard someone say – 'I'll swap you three Noël Cowards for one Jessie Matthews'.

Had he ever told Miss Matthews?

> Yes, she didn't speak to me for three weeks, she was so pleased with herself.
>
> Television interview (1968)

As an actor, he was well aware of his range and the need to stay within it. Shakespeare intrigued him, and many of his plays took their titles from Shakespearean quotations – *Blithe Spirit, Present Laughter, This Happy Breed* - but to *act* the Bard was quite another matter:

> I was offered Hamlet five times . . . I just knew that the day I declaimed 'To be or not to be' in public, it would be the death of me.
>
> Daily Mail (1969)

Would he contemplate it in the future?

> I think I've left it a bit late! I might play the Nurse in *Romeo and Juliet*.

He also thought he might be 'rather good as Madame Arcati'!

Having played King Magnus in Shaw's *The Apple Cart* during Coronation Year . . .

> I am not at all certain that in the future when I write a part I shall not write myself a king; it really is so satisfactory to have all the other characters standing up so often.
>
> *Diaries* (1953)

There was a fair amount of Noël Coward in Garry Essendine – with a welcome splash of self-deprecation . . .

> GARRY: I'm always acting – watching myself go by – that's what's so horrible – I see myself all the time eating, drinking, loving, suffering . . . my life is not my own . . . I belong to the public and to my work.
>
> *Present Laughter* (1939)

To Rattigan after lukewarm reception for *The Sleeping Prince* . . .

> Don't worry, Terence, I not only fuck up some of my plays by writing them but I frequently fuck them up by acting in them as well.

And Coward was perfectly realistic about his relative stature as an actor . . .

> If you were to put me on a stage with Laurence Olivier, John Gielgud and Ralph Richardson, they would be acting me off the stage and out of the auditorium – but everyone in the audience would be looking at me.
>
> To his godson, Daniel Massey (attributed)

Although many considered him the definitive performer of his own songs, the verdict was not unanimous. A critic reviewing his 1951 cabaret début at the Café de Paris accused him of 'massacring' his material. If so, Coward declared in his *Diaries*:

> It was the most profitable massacre since the St. Valentine's Day massacre.

Nonetheless, he had no illusions about his technical vocal accomplishments:

> It is a composer's voice. It has considerable range but no tone, little music, but lots of meaning.

:::   :::   :::

> I can't sing but I know how to, which is quite different.
>
> *Observer* (1969)

Cabaret in London and Las Vegas was to lead to television, but the technical aspects of this new miracle medium, of course, were quite beyond him . . .

> . . . my brain shudders at the very idea.
>
> *Future Indefinite* (1954)

As early as 1947 he was inclined to dismiss the new medium . . .

> What I have learned so far is that, apart from a few special personalities and talents, the standard of entertainment is poor, the lighting unpredictable, and the commercial emphasis very overstressed. I have seen to date few evidences of imagination in production and no sense of experimentation.
>
> *Diaries* (1955)

. . . but when he found himself having to tackle it professionally, he discovered all it needed was his usual discipline . . .

> The TV spectacular I am going to do with Mary Martin will be completely spontaneous. The kind of spontaneity I like best – the kind that comes after five weeks' rehearsal.
>
> (1955)

In that same year he was forced to admit that 'this curious medium' had its artistic advantages – even for a middle-aged playwright:

> The cutting of my plays down for television is certainly a salutary experience, and I believe that the next time I embark on a full-length play for the theatre, I shall find that I have profited by it. I shall have learned, for instance, to dispense with amusing irrelevancies that have no direct bearing on the story and to get back to my original method of saying what I have to say in as few lines as possible with a minimum of atmospheric padding and linguistic flourishes.
>
> *Diaries* (1956)

Coward had a career-long feud with dramatic critics. Having received virtually unqualified praise in his early twenties, he found himself an early victim of media 'deconstruction' for much of the rest of his life. His crusade of retaliation didn't help matters:

> Criticism and Bolshevism have one thing in common. They both seek to pull down that which they could never build.
>
> (1925)

:::   :::   :::

I have always been fond of them [critics] . . . I think it is so frightfully clever of them to go night after night to the theatre and know so little about it.

⁑ ⁑ ⁑

I don't know what makes them so vitriolic; I suppose it's my continued success and something about my personality that infuriates them, in which case I fear they will have to get on with it.

Diaries (1959)

⁑ ⁑ ⁑

Alas, in public life it is often necessary to take the rough with the smooth, and occasionally with the rough.

'A Richer Dust'

⁑ ⁑ ⁑

If I had really cared about the critics, I would have shot myself in the Twenties.

Play Parade Volume 4 (1954)

⁑ ⁑ ⁑

I can take any amount of criticism, so long as it is unqualified praise.

Press interview

⁑ ⁑ ⁑

'I have a great friend who is a journalist,' I said.
'She's a darling.'

'Then she must be a very bad journalist,' snapped
Buddha. 'No good journalist could go on being a
darling even if she started as one.'

Pomp and Circumstance (1960)

⁝ ⁝ ⁝

Newspaper reporting, either of events or people,
depends for its effectiveness on superficial
observation and snap judgements; speed and brevity
are essential and there is rarely time for subtle
analysis or true assessment of character. Usually, in
the case of a celebrity, the label has been fixed and
the clichés set for years.

(1952)

⁝ ⁝ ⁝

The critics described *Private Lives* variously as
'tenuous, thin, brittle, gossamer, iridescent and
delightfully daring'. All of which connoted in the
public mind cocktails, repartee and irreverent allusions
to copulation, thereby causing a gratifying number of
respectable people to queue up at the box office.

Play Parade Volume 1 (1934)

Even so, it would be hypocritical to pretend that good reviews did not stroke
a writer's feathers the right way. Certainly they did for Evan Lorrimer,
Noël's novelist in 'What Mad Pursuit?'

Such allusions . . . are immensely agreeable.
Unimportant, perhaps, in their essence, but in their

implication very important indeed. Just as millions of little coral animals in so many years construct a barrier reef against the sea, so can these small accolades, over a period of time, build, if not quite a barrier reef, at least a fortification against the waves of oblivion.

But Coward remained philosophical:

> For who is to say with any certainty which of an artist's works are his best? Everyone knows that contemporary judgment is not to be relied upon and in fact it is a fairly safe rule to take the opposite view to the current one. Even Time will not tell, for an artist is sometimes remembered and loved for his more popular works rather than his best . . .
>
> Magazine interview (1939)

And throughout his career he remained ruthlessly *self*-critical . . .

> I seem in later years to have lost my gift for economy.
>
> *Diaries* (1955)

The last show that Coward ever saw was a gala performance of the New York compilation revue *Oh, Coward!* Asked if he was laughing at the lines, he replied:

> One doesn't laugh at his own jokes.
>
> (1973)

But perhaps the line that best sums up Coward on theatre was this one:

> If you're a star, you should behave like one. I always have.
>
> *Sunday Times* (1969)

PART TWO

⋮⋮⋮   ⋮⋮⋮   ⋮⋮⋮

'A Marvellous Party'

The English class system was a recurrent theme in Coward's work. Although his own origins were lower-middle class, the public persona he created enabled him to mingle with all levels of society.

> The cream of the aristocracy mingles with the clotted cream of the (theatrical) profession.
>
> Introduction to Three Plays

⁙   ⁙   ⁙

> I think social distinctions are very important because they make a balance.
>
> Interview with Edgar Lustgarten (1972)

And he added somewhat defensively:

> If I were only interested in the Ritz and Royalty could I have written *Brief Encounter* and *This Happy Breed*?

His perception ensured that he saw all of its strata clearly and took none of them entirely seriously. There was the Landed Gentry:

> *The Stately Homes of England,*
> *How beautiful they stand,*
> *To prove the upper classes*
> *Have still the upper hand;*

Though the fact that they have to be rebuilt
And frequently mortgaged to the hilt
Is inclined to take the gilt
Off the gingerbread . . .

'The Stately Homes of England' – *Operette* (1938)

⠿   ⠿   ⠿

AMANDA: Whose yacht is that?
ELYOT: The Duke of Westminster's I expect. It
always is.

Private Lives (1936)

But there was aristocracy and aristocracy. Observing a mixed bag of minor honourables at a society wedding long after the Royals had departed, Coward remarked to a fellow guest, Richard Burton:

Here come the riff-raff.

And then, of course, there were the Poor Rich . . . Considering his friends, the Westminsters:

Stone walls do not a prison make nor iron bars a cage, but millions of pounds can make, very subtly, both.

(1962)

During his lifetime, Coward's beady eye was always busy 'watching Society scampering past' and observing its mores shift. In the 1920s it was perfectly permissible – even de rigeur – to appear socially frivolous:

EUSTACE: The only thing more expensive than
hunting is virtue.

The Young Idea (1921)

⁜　⁜　⁜

CICELY: I do wish you wouldn't despise my husband
so, Roddy, it isn't good form.

The Young Idea (1921)

⁜　⁜　⁜

JENNIFER: I have never been able to take anything
seriously after eleven o'clock in the morning.

The Young Idea (1921)

⁜　⁜　⁜

If it's rissoles, I shan't dress – a rule I made in 1929
and to which I still strictly adhere.

(1956)

And the world could safely be populated with social butterflies and chinless
wonders – a species that could still be occasionally sighted years later.
Coward recalled meeting 'a startled young man fresh from Oxford with
over-eager teeth' as late as 1953 (*Diaries*).

The war, though, had changed all that and the values of the post-war
world were not particularly to Coward's liking:

FELICITY: One of the worst aspects of modern
English life is that so many of one's friends have to
work and they're so bad at it.

Relative Values (1951)

⁜　⁜　⁜

CRESTWELL (THE BUTLER): Above all I drink to the
final inglorious disintegration of the most unlikely
dream that ever troubled the foolish heart of man –
Social Equality!

Relative Values (1951)

After all, weren't we *all* the Bourgeoisie now . . . ?

Long live the Bourgeoisie!
We oil our bats
And we clean our clubs,
We're democrats
In the local pubs.
We like Britannia to rule
the waves
We don't believe that the
waves are ruled by
slaves.
Let the 'Workers' unite,
Let the classes fight
We'll be glad to referee
(From our seat on the
sidelines)
Esprit de corps, lads
Wins every war, lads.
Long live the Bourgeoisie!

'Long Live the Bourgeoisie!'
from *Hoi Polloi* (1947)
– unproduced musical

There were – or should be – certain fixed points even in a changing world and over the years Coward would seek to define them:

> Class was class and there was no getting away from it.
>
> 'The Kindness of Mrs. Radcliffe'

⁝　　⁝　　⁝

> EVAN: Manners are the outward expression of expert interior decoration.
>
> *Long Island Sound* (1947)

On taste:

> It can be vulgar, but it must never be embarrassing.
>
> John Lahr, *Coward the Playwright* (1982)

⁝　　⁝　　⁝

> Style in everything demands discipline.
>
> *Daily Mail* (1966)

In retrospect he had to admit that his own sense of style had not always been completely impeccable . . .

> My own audition apparel was usually a navy blue suit with a coloured shirt, tie, socks, and handkerchief to match. I had not learned then that an exact duplication of colours ill becomes the well-dressed man.
>
> *Present Indicative* (1937)

In the 1950s Noël made one of his rare appearances in an advertisement. The Gillette Company, launching their new 'Aristocrat' razor blade, asked him to define 'Style'. His quirkish reply was . . .

A candy-striped jeep

Jane Austen

Cassius Clay

THE TIMES before it changed

Danny LaRue

Charleston, South Carolina

'Monsieur' de Givenchy

A zebra (but NOT a zebra crossing)

Evading boredom

Gertrude Lawrence

The Paris Opera House

White

A seagull

A Brixham trawler

Margot Fonteyn

Any Cole Porter song

English pageantry

Marlene's voice

Lingfield has a *tiny* bit

⁛　⁛　⁛

Conceit is an outward manifestation of inferiority.

The Times (1969)

⁛　⁛　⁛

I absolutely loathe champagne. Have since I was twenty.

New York Herald Tribune
(1963)

⊞   ⊞   ⊞

I've got to go out and be social,
I've got to be bright
And extremely polite
And refrain from becoming too loose or too tight
And I mustn't impose conversational blight
On the dolt on my left
And the fool on my right.
I must really be very attractive tonight
As I have to go out and be social.

Unpublished verse

When you come right down to it, he concluded quite early, each of us had to decide who we wanted to be and then set about creating that persona. He certainly devoted his own life to doing so:

LEO: It's all a question of masks, really; brittle, painted masks. We all wear them as a form of protection; modern life forces us to. We must have some means of shielding our timid, shrinking souls from the glare of civilisation.

Design For Living (1932)

Of course, for the true Social Animal, a certain amount of civilised glare was inevitable. After all, there were the inevitable parties to go to . . . and one in particular. Coward never forgot the 1930s party in the south of France to which hostess Elsa Maxwell invited him. When he arrived, he found that he was expected to entertain the guests. He firmly declined, then enshrined the occasion in song:

> *I went to a marvellous party,*
> *We played the most wonderful game,*
> *Maureen disappeared*
> *And came back in a beard*
> *And we all had to guess her name!*
> *We talked about growing old gracefully*
> *And Elsie who's seventy-four*
> *Said, 'A, it's a question of being sincere,*
> *And B, if you're supple you've nothing to fear'.*
> *Then she swung upside down from a glass chandelier,*
> *I couldn't have liked it more.*

'I Went to a Marvellous Party'
from Set to Music (1939)

And as the cocktails flowed at every social occasion worth the name, the talk would inevitably turn to the Arts. No matter what the year, there was the endless debate over the modern novel:

MRS. ASTON-HOOPER: I get so tired of the usual modern novels. They nearly always end with the hero having been married forty years to the heroine, gazing down the vista of his life and saying – 'I wonder', until a dotted line cuts his rather aimless musings short.

The Unattainable (1918) – unpublished play

Whatever he chose to say in his plays, in private life he was positively puritanical:

> If there's anything I hate in modern novels it is this sex obsession, this pseudo-tough realism in which every sexual depravity is intimately dissected. It drags one straight back to Jane Austen.
>
> Interview (1968)

⁘   ⁘   ⁘

> It was sheer pornography. The heroine was a lesbian and a drunkard – but she finished up a nun, which was meant to mean, I suppose, that she was really all right. There was one tremendous chapter that was nothing but filth: it made me think of the dedication – 'To my dear wife, Lillian, without whom this book would not have been possible.'

He firmly believed that the sexiest book ever written was *Madame Bovary*, since it proved you could achieve any erotic effect you wished without having to resort to four letter words. And he had strong views on what he read and those who wrote it. Of Henry James – ('the King of exquisitely phrased verbosity') – more in sorrow than in anger:

> . . . poor Mr. James who trudges and writhes and wriggles through jungles of verbiage to describe a cucumber sandwich.
>
> *Diaries* (1957)

Then, of course, there was the inevitable Oscar Wilde. In the early 1950s, Noël had found the task of turning *Lady Windermere's Fan* into *After The Ball* a more difficult assignment than he had bargained for. Both men were great and original wits but their sensibilities were very different. What one

· 55 ·

liked the other loathed. As a colleague of Coward's put it – it was like having two celebrities at the same dinner party, competing for attention. Some years later the Coward mind was firmly made up:

> It is extraordinary indeed that such a posing, artificial old queen should have written one of the greatest comedies in the English language. In my opinion it was the only thing of the least *importance* that he did write.
>
> *Diaries* (1962)

In 1961 Noël wrote a series of articles for the *Sunday Times*, castigating, among others, the currently fashionable 'Kitchen Sink' playwrights. Not surprisingly, since his own reputation was in decline at the time, his motives were questioned. Nonetheless, they were views he has held consistently for some time.

Of John Osborne:

> I cannot believe that this writer, the first of the 'angry young men', was ever really angry at all. Dissatisfied, perhaps, and certainly envious and, to a degree, talented, but no more than that. No leader of thought and ideas, a conceited, calculating young man blowing a little trumpet.
>
> *Diaries* (1959)

One of the contemporary writers he did admire was Peter Shaffer, who had just written *The Royal Hunt of the Sun*:

> The difference between Peter Shaffer and all the Osbornes and Weskers is that he has no hatred in his heart and no partisan axe to grind. He writes compassionately about human beings. He also has more than a touch of poetry. I only wish he would write more.
>
> *Diaries* (1964)

After hating the early work Noël became a convert to Harold Pinter . . .

> I think I'm now on Pinter's wavelength. He is at least
> a genuine original. I don't think he could write in any
> other way if he tried. *The Caretaker,* on the face of it,
> is everything I hate most in the theatre; squalor,
> repetition, lack of action, but somehow it seizes hold
> of you . . . Nothing happens except that somehow it
> does.

He had mixed views of American playwright, Edward Albee. Having found *Who's Afraid of Virginia Woolf?* (1963) 'fine, scathing, sublimely acted', he found *Tiny Alice* (1965) 'so nearly good and yet so maddeningly pretentious' and wrote to the playwright a few days later from Jamaica to clarify his reaction . . .

> I have a profound respect for your rich talent . . .
> Expert use of language is to me a perpetual joy. You
> use it expertly, all right, but I fear, too self-
> indulgently. Your duty to me as a playgoer and a
> reader is to explain whatever truths you are dealing
> with as lucidly and accurately. I refuse to be fobbed
> off with a sort of metaphysical. 'What's My Line?'
> Let me hear from you. An ordinary love letter will
> do!
>
> Letter (1965)

Years before, he had failed to fully appreciate Arthur Miller. After a performance of *Death of a Salesman* he heard someone gush that what they had just seen was not a play but an 'experience' . . .

> I wish it had been a play.

Then there was art – both ancient, as on seeing the Venus de Milo:

> It's only what's to be expected if you will go on
> biting your nails.

Attributed

. . . and modern (a particular Coward *bête noire*):

> SEBASTIEN: I don't think anyone knows about
> painting any more. Art, like human nature, has got
> out of hand.

Nude With Violin (1954)

After reading Wilenski's book *Lives of the Impressionists:*

> Really no burlesque however extravagant could equal
> the phrases he uses to describe the 'Abstract' boys.
> Quite a lot of it is completely unintelligible. He talks
> a great deal of 'emotive force' and 'lyrical colour' and
> 'constant functional forms', etc., and after he has
> described a picture in approximately these terms you
> turn to a coloured plate and look at a square lady with
> three breasts and a guitar up her crotch.

Diaries (1954)

⁙　　⁙　　⁙

> He's running a temperature and his chest looks like a
> bad Matisse.

Pomp and Circumstance (1960)

⁙　　⁙　　⁙

Perhaps I was frightened by a Bellini Madonna when I was a tiny child.

Present Indicative (1937)

Wagner and his works crop up frequently in Coward's critical litany ('Not a *tremendous* Wagnerian on account of getting fidgety' . . . 'I wish he'd get on with it') and *Parsifal* came in for particular scrutiny. Having seen *Camelot* (1955):

It's about as long as *Parsifal* and not as funny.

⸬　　⸬　　⸬

ELENA: My husband was an operatic tenor. He sang very loudly, particularly in *Norma*. I think that was what finished him.

Pacific 1860 (1946)

⸬　　⸬　　⸬

GILDA: People are wrong when they say that the opera isn't what it used to be. It *is* what it used to be – that's what's wrong with it.

Design For Living (1932)

Nor did eighteenth-century music appeal. Take Mozart . . .

All too often it sounds like a Pekinese peeing on a mink rug.

Quoted by Julian Slade

⸬　　⸬　　⸬

I don't like good music . . . I can't bear Mozart. I know I'm missing a lot, but that can't be helped.

Nor did many composers fare much better . . .

Though Wolfgang Mozart wrote The Magic Flute he
Alas, alas composed Cosi Fan Tutte . . .
But then poor Donizetti
Was likewise not
Too hot
At choosing libretti.
Then there are those Rosenkavaliers and Fledermauses
Written by all those Strausses
Which play to crowded houses
And, to me, are louses.

'Opera Notes', *Collected Verse* (1984)

⁙　⁙　⁙

B: She doesn't really mind what it is. She's perfectly happy so long as she can let her emeralds glitter to Chopin.

A: I've never heard Chopin there. They nearly always play Brahms with woebegone faces and India-rubber collars.

The Unattainable (1918) – unpublished play

⁙　⁙　⁙

STELLA: I always had my suspicions about Derek. There was something in the way he played the piano.

JUDY: Come now, Stella. He did at least play the piano beautifully.

STELLA: Too much Debussy.

Age Cannot Wither (1967) – unproduced play

⁙　⁙　⁙

Having been deafened by Wagnerian bassoons
I much prefer these ultra-British
Rather skittish
Little tunes.

'The Girl Who Came to Supper' (1963) – unpublished song

⁙　⁙　⁙

There has never yet been composed a piece of classical music that was not too long.

Diaries (1964)

His own musical taste ran more to the romantic and melodic. ('I love Verdi and Donizetti and all those boys') which did not stop him tweaking them when the fancy took him . . .

> *I think we must face the fact*
> *That Carmen by Bizet*
> *Is no more Spanish than the Champs Elysées*

And . . .

> *We must admit that every hurdy-gurdy*
> *Owes a deep debt of gratitude*
> *To Giuseppe Verdi*

'Not Yet the Dodo'

Coward enjoyed the arts, and the associated 'high society' lifestyle. But he couldn't always keep up with the changing scene. After the initial sense of loss, he was inclined to wonder whether, after all, nostalgia was quite what it used to be:

It was a *nostalgie du temps perdu* and I wasn't somehow all that sorry when the *temps* were *perdu*.

Diaries (1966)

PART THREE

::: ::: :::

'Mad Dogs and Englishmen'

To the end of his days Coward remained a flag-waving patriot, even if the England he celebrated had become largely a figment of his memory. In many ways he was a Victorian stranded in another era and suffering from a malaise he would term 'Twentieth Century Blues':

> *In this strange*
>   *illusion,*
> *Chaos and confusion,*
> *People seem to lose their*
>   *way.*
> *What is there to strive for,*
> *Love or keep alive for? Say –*
> *Hey, hey, call it a day.*
> *Blues, nothing to win or to lose.*
> *It's getting me down.*
> *Blues, I've got those weary*
> *Twentieth Century Blues.*
>
>   'Twentieth Century Blues' from
>   *Cavalcade* (1931)

Personally he needed to believe that the Old Country could find a new purpose. In *Cavalcade* he has the heroine (Jane Marryot), towards the end of a long life, give the New Year Toast to the Future that she has given every year:

JANE: Let's drink to the hope that one day this country of ours, which we love so much, will find dignity and greatness and peace again.

· 65 ·

During the 1930s he came to despise Neville Chamberlain and all those who trusted the theory of appeasement. Frank Gibbons addresses his infant grandson at the end of *This Happy Breed* (1939):

You belong to a race that's been bossy for years and the reason it's held on as long as it has is that nine times out of ten it's behaved decently and treated people right. Just lately, I'll admit, we've been giving at the knees a bit and letting people down who trusted us and allowing noisy little men to bully us with a lot of guns and bombs and aeroplanes. But don't worry – that won't last – the people themselves, the ordinary people like you and me, know something better than all the fussy old politicians put together – we know what we belong to, where we come from, and where we're going. We may not know it in our brains, but we know it in our roots. And we know another thing, too, and it's this. We 'aven't lived and died and struggled all these hundreds of years to get decency and justice and freedom for ourselves without being prepared to fight fifty wars if need be – to keep 'em.

⁑　⁑　⁑

To most people this war has been an absolute blessing. It's not only provided them with an all-absorbing topic of conversation but furnished their empty minds with frequent opportunities for indulging in maudlin sentiment and cheap patriotism.

⁑　⁑　⁑

She was too interested in women's suffrage . . . and when war broke out and there was nothing more exciting for women to fight for than margarine – the shock killed her!

But, on occasion, overt emotion from the supposedly cynical Mr Coward raised a number of eyebrows and questions about his sincerity – a situation he had aggravated by his first-night speech:

'. . . in spite of the troublous times we are living in, it is still pretty exciting to be English' . . . quite true, quite sincere; I felt it strongly, but I rather wished I hadn't said it, hadn't popped it on to the top of *Cavalcade* like a paper-cap.

⁂   ⁂   ⁂

The rumour was fairly general that I had written it with my tongue in my cheek, probably in bed, wearing a silk dressing-gown and shaking with cynical laughter.

Present Indicative (1937)

With the arrival of the Second World War it became Noël's ambition to write the definitive war song – something that would match Ivor Novello's 'Keep The Home Fires Burning' from the first 'war to end wars'. One morning in 1941, sitting in a bomb-damaged London railway station after a particularly bad blitz, the sight of a small wild flower bravely struggling to survive seemed to symbolise something about the city and the people he loved so much:

London Pride has been handed down to us.
London Pride is a flower that's free.
London Pride means our own dear town to us,

And our pride it forever will be . . .
Cockney feet
Mark the beat of history.
Every street
Pins a memory down.
Nothing ever can quite replace
The grace of London Town.

'London Pride' (1941)

It was a sentiment he was to express in words (and often music) for the next thirty years:

I was a flagrant, unabashed sentimentalist and likely
to remain so until the end of my days. I did love
England and all it stood for. I loved its follies and
apathies and curious streaks of genius; I loved
standing to attention for 'God Save the King'; I
loved British courage, British humour, and British
understatement . . . I loved the people – the ordinary,
the extraordinary, the good, the bad, the indifferent,
and what is more I belonged to that exasperating,
weather-sodden little island with its uninspired
cooking, its muddled thinking and its unregenerate
pride, and it belonged to me, whether it liked it or
not.

Future Indefinite (1954)

⁕   ⁕   ⁕

I *am* England and England is me.

Sunday Express (1965)

He most certainly did like it, even though he had always seen it warts and all. Even in his own early twenties he had catalogued what he saw as a dangerous *ennui* of the post-war younger generation that was knock, knock, knocking at the door . . .

In lives of leisure
The craze for pleasure
Steadily grows.
Cocktails and laughter
But what comes after?
Nobody knows.

'Poor Little Rich Girl' from *On With the Dance* (1925)

⁂   ⁂   ⁂

No more the moon
On the still Lagoon
Can please the young enchanted,
They must have this
And they must have that
And they take it all for granted.
They hitch their star
To a cocktail bar
Which is all they really wanted . . .

'The Lido Beach' from *This Year of Grace!* (1928)

One thing never disappointed – the charm of London Town . . .

London – is a little bit of all right,
Nobody can deny that's true . . .
London – is a place where you can call right
Round and have a cosy cup of tea,
If you're fed right up and got your tail right down

London town
Is a wonderful place to be.

From *The Girl Who Came To Supper* (1963)

Perhaps, though, there were one or two small improvements we could make:

We downtrodden British must learn to be skittish
And give an impression of devil-may-care . . .

'Don't Make Fun of the Fair' (1951)

⁛　　⁛　　⁛

We British are a peculiar breed
Undemonstrative on the whole.
It takes a very big shock indeed
To dent our maddening self-control . . .

Our far-flung Empire imposed new rules
And lasted a century or so
Until, engrossed with our football pools
We shrugged our shoulders and let it go.

'Not Yet the Dodo' (1967)

⁛　　⁛　　⁛

LAURA:　Do you know, I believe we should all behave
quite differently if we lived in a warm, sunny
climate all the time. We shouldn't be so withdrawn
and shy and difficult.

Brief Encounter (1945)

As the years went by, though, he found it progressively harder to equate 'swinging sixties' England with the *Great* Britain he had known. But as late as 1957 and well after Suez he could still say:

> The British Empire was a great and wonderful social, economic and even spiritual experiment, and all the parlour pinks and eager, ill-informed intellectuals cannot convince me to the contrary . . . At the present moment England is in a state of almost complete subservience to America and for the worst possible reason, that America is the richer. I, who genuinely love America and Americans, cannot ignore their only too obvious naivety in world diplomacy.
>
> *Diaries* (1957)

In 1963 he attended the annual Battle of Britain dinner and found himself asking:

> What was it that I so minded about twenty-three years ago? An ideal? An abstract patriotism? What? . . . I wanted suddenly to stand up and shout . . . 'Let's face the truth. The England we knew and loved was betrayed at Munich, revived for one short year in 1940 and was supreme in adversity, and now no longer exists.' That last great war was our valediction. It will never happen again.
>
> *Diaries* (1963)

⋮   ⋮   ⋮

> An Englishman is the highest example of a human being who is a free man.
>
> Interview with Hunter Davies (1969)

⠿   ⠿   ⠿

I continue to tell foreigners how great we are. Before
I die, I would like once again to be able to believe
this myself.

Sunday Express (1965)

He was, by his own admission, 'a cosy Royal snob' and became close and
genuine friends with several members of the Royal Family. When Graham
Payn thanked the Queen Mother for attending Noël's memorial service in
Westminster Abbey in 1984, she replied simply: 'He was my friend.' Noël
liked nothing better than the 'theatre' of Royalty – the marching military
bands, the salutes, the flags waving . . .

> *Everyone in London likes a damn good show,*
> *A properly planned procession or parade.*
> *It's not because we're snobs*
> *But we like to be sure the Nobs*
> *With all that kow-towing*
> *And bobbing and bowing*
> *Are bloody well doing their jobs.*
> *Flags against the sky.*
> *Horses galloping by,*
> *Yards and yards of Guards*
> *In their golden braid.*
> *We'll stand in the sun,*
> *We'll stand in the rain*
> *Or fog or sleet or snow,*
> *For Londoners like a damn good show.*

'Damn Good Show'
from *Hoi Polloi* (1947)
– unproduced musical

⠿   ⠿   ⠿

There is little sense in having a constitutional monarchy and not being a cosy royal snob.

Diaries (1957)

Patriotic to the last, Coward loved both England and the English:

It merely occurred to me that I belonged to a most remarkable race. In later years I have seen no reason

· 73 ·

to revise this opinion. I am quite aware of our shortcomings, perhaps even more so than more impartial observers because I have suffered from them personally. . . However, so much as I may loathe this and that and the other, it is what I love that really counts, and what I love about my country is really quite simple. I love its basic integrity, an integrity formed over hundreds of years by indigenous humour, courage and common-sense.

Past Conditional (1965)

PART FOUR

::: ::: :::

'Sail Away'

We British are an island race,
The sea lies all around us,
And visitors from other lands,
With different sets of different glands,
Bewilder and astound us.

Conversation Piece (1934)

Along with his strong sense of patriotism, Noël sometimes displayed a suspicion, even a dislike, of those from other countries. To start with, there was our age-old sparring partner across the Channel:

There's always something fishy about the French!
We've a sinister suspicion
That behind their savoir-faire
They share
A common contempt
For every mother's son of us.
Tho' they smile and smirk
We know they're out for dirty work . . .
Every wise and thoroughly worldly wench
Knows there's always something fishy about the French!

Conversation Piece (1934)

Although we may not be entirely blameless ourselves:

Foreigners' immorality may make us look askance,
Though we are not above it if we get the slightest chance.
What is it makes an Englishman enjoy himself in France?

Or, if you looked across that other stretch of sea:

> The Irish behave exactly as they
> have been portrayed as behaving
> for years. Charming, soft-voiced,
> quarrelsome, Priest-ridden,
> feckless and happily devoid of the
> slightest integrity in our stodgy
> English sense of the word.
>
> On his first visit to Dublin (1960)

Then, of course, there were the Germans.
Coward's side-swipe at them early in the war
was totally misread by many and censored for
a while until the irony was firmly established.
An exception was Winston Churchill who 'liked it
so much that I had to sing it to him seven times in
one evening'.

> *Don't let's be beastly to the*
>   *Germans*
> *When the age of peace and plenty*
>   *has begun.*
> *We must send them steel and oil and coal and everything*
>   *they need*
> *For their peaceable intentions can be always guaranteed.*
> *Let's employ with them a sort of 'strength through joy'*
>   *with them,*
> *They're better than us at honest manly fun.*
> *Let's let them feel they're swell again and bomb us all to*
>   *hell again,*
> *But don't let's be beastly to the Hun.*
>
> 'Don't Let's Be Beastly to the Germans' (1943)

⁘ ⁘ ⁘

The Germans have been aggressive, cruel and humourless all through their dismal history, and I find it quite impossible to forgive them, however politic it may be considered to do so. They are a horrid, neurotic race and always have been and always will be and, to my mind, none of their contributions to science, literature and music compensates for their turgid emotionalism and unparalleled capacity for torturing their fellow creatures.

Diaries (1955)

The Austrians, on the other hand, he always found to be 'sweet people but overmusical':

When we wake in the morning, the very first thing
That we Austrians do is to sing and to sing.
Tho' on every occasion our voices excel
In a National crisis we yodel as well.

Operette (1938)

⁛　　⁛　　⁛

ISOBEL: When she was seventeen she was sent to Geneva to be finished.
CHERRY-MAY: I should think Geneva'd be enough to finish anybody.

Nude With Violin (1956)

Yet Switzerland was a country that seemed to appeal to him from the first. In early 1939 he visited Lausanne and spent a happy time 'on the bonny, bonny banks of Lac Leman' on which he observed there was 'no lack *des cygnes*'. And in 1968 he could add . . .

I now live in Switzerland where I have a spectacular view overlooking an absolutely ravishing tax advantage.

Sunday Times

Then there were the Russians, whom he first met *in situ* in 1939 . . .

I know it is an accepted theory that the English take their pleasures sadly, but as far as I could see the Soviets didn't seem to take them at all, or perhaps there weren't any to take.

Future Indefinite (1954)

Despite his reservations, he saw earlier than most of his countrymen the sense of a single European entity – even though he cloaked his comment in a jibe . . .

I hoped we *would* go into the Common Market for the simple but valid reason that Beaverbrook was so dead against it. This I have always found a fairly safe hoe to furrow, or is it furrow to hoe?

Diaries (1963)

Most other parts of the world, it seems, he could take or leave:

*Saint Petersburg, of course, has flair
But can be dull without the snow,
Berlin is much too polyglot
And Rome in summer is dreadfully hot,
Vienna makes one ill at ease
With those vocal Viennese,
And Athens with its ruins and fleas
Is far too Greek.*

After the Ball (1954)

⠿ ⠿ ⠿

LEO: I've never been able to understand why the Japanese are such a cheerful race. All that hissing and grinning on the brink of destruction.

OTTO: The Japanese don't mind destruction a bit; they like it, it's part of their upbringing. They're delighted with death. Look at the way they kill themselves on the most whimsical of pretexts.

LEO: I always thought Madame Butterfly was over-hasty.

Design For Living (1932)

⠿ ⠿ ⠿

JUDY: Italians are naturally cruel, I'm afraid. Look how they whack away at those wretched donkeys in Capri.

Age Cannot Wither (1967) – unproduced play

⠿ ⠿ ⠿

She said, 'They're just high-spirited, like all Italians are. And most of them have a great deal more to offer than Papa'.

'A Bar on the Piccola Marina' (1954)

⠿ ⠿ ⠿

AMANDA: I know what the Hungarians are, too.

ELYOT: What are they?

AMANDA: Very wistful. It's all those pretzels, I shouldn't wonder.

Private Lives (1930)

⁂　⁂　⁂

SHOLTO: There's always a political crisis in Bulgaria, the same as there's always haggis in Scotland. It's traditional.

The Young Idea (1921)

In New Zealand he attended a Maori ceremony . . .

I was presented to the chiefs and the local belles, with whom I rubbed noses; this was damp but convivial. Then came the entertainment, which consisted of native songs and dances, slightly spoiled for me by the fact that the male dancers wore ordinary grey flannel trousers under their straw skirts, which, I thought, vitiated the primitive barbarity of the occasion.

Future Indefinite (1954)

⁂　⁂　⁂

They all insist that South America's exotic Whereas it couldn't be more boring if it tried.

'Nina' (1945)

⁂　⁂　⁂

The one place that fascinated and frustrated him in equal measure from his first sight of it in 1921 was America:

> *I like America,*
> *I have played around*
> *Every slappy-happy hunting ground*
> *But I find America – okay*
> *And come what may*
> *Give me a holiday*
> *In the good old U. S. A.*
> *I like America,*
> *Every scrap of it,*
> *All the sentimental crap of it.*
> *I've been about a bit*
> *But I must admit*
> *That I didn't know the half of it*
> *Till I hit the U. S. A.*

'I Like America' from *Ace of Clubs* (1949)

⁂　⁂　⁂

'Krispy-Kuts' will make his every meal a passionate experience, while 'Maltofoam' will ensure an ecstatic old age for his mother because it is 'The Beer with a Kick to it'.

Australia Visited (1940)

But while he might like *America* most of the time, he never ceased to be amazed at the more bizarre aspects of Americans and Americana in general.

I love the weight of American Sunday newspapers. Pulling them up off the floor is good for the figure.

Dick Richards, *The Wit of Noël Coward* (1968)

⁞   ⁞   ⁞

Without America we should have no Coca-Cola, no Marilyn Monroe and hardly any really good literature about sex.

⁞   ⁞   ⁞

Verbal diarrhoea is a major defect in many American writers. They have learnt assiduously *too many words* and they wish you to know that they know *far more words* than other people and, what is more, long and complicated words. This adolescent crowing becomes quite deafening sometimes and gets between them and what they are trying to say . . .

Diaries (1955)

⁞   ⁞   ⁞

'It's strange to find an American who really loves Jane Austen, isn't it?'

'I don't know,' replied Lola dryly. 'She has acquired quite an international reputation lately, having got into the paperbacks.'

'Bon Voyage'

⁞   ⁞   ⁞

American women mostly have their clothes arranged for them. And their faces, too, I think.

Dick Richards, *The Wit of Noël Coward* (1968)

⁞   ⁞   ⁞

Americans love ice and hate cold water and so the swimming pools are as hot as *bouillabaisse*.

Dick Richards, *The Wit of Noël Coward* (1968)

⁙   ⁙   ⁙

It is really surprising how many American adults . . . have plunged into psychiatry so that their egos have grown inwards, like toenails.

Diaries (1962)

⁙   ⁙   ⁙

I hate the United States' behaviour to English, with such words as 'hospitalized' and 'togetherness'. And how about 'trained nurse'? Absurd. What in heaven's name is the use of an *un*trained nurse?

To an American reporter

⁙   ⁙   ⁙

NORMA: After all, we all love our country and are proud of it – it is the last refuge of peace and freedom in the world today – but you must admit that, once you've exhausted Palm Beach and California, there aren't many places to go.

Time Remembered (1941) – unproduced play

⁙   ⁙   ⁙

MELODY: Americans have a passion for speed . . . and yet no idea of time whatsoever – it's most extraordinary.

Time Remembered (1941) – unproduced play

⁝⁝⁝   ⁝⁝⁝   ⁝⁝⁝

MAXIE: Buffet lunches . . . are always a drain on one's vitality. They call them fork luncheons over here, you know. I always think it sounds vaguely pornographic.

Time Remembered (1941) – unproduced play

⁜　⁜　⁜

In America they have to be told what to enjoy and
what to avoid, not only in the theatre but in every
phase of life. They are told by television what to eat,
drink, or smoke, what cars to buy and what laxatives
and sanitary towels to use. They are allowed to
choose, admittedly from not too glamorous a
selection, what gods to worship. The power of
individual thought has been atrophied in them by the
incessant onslaughts of commercialism.

Diaries (1957)

But even so, when all was said and done . . .

> *I like America*
> *Its Society*
> *Offers infinite variety*
> *And come what may*
> *I shall return some day*
> *To the good old U. S. A.*

And he frequently did.

Travel was Coward's safety valve. When his pressured professional life
caught up with him – which it frequently did – his recourse was to embark
on a long trip to recharge his batteries.

I have never liked living anywhere all the year
round.

⁜　⁜　⁜

When the storm clouds are riding through a winter sky
Sail away – sail away.
When the love-light is fading in your sweetheart's eye
Sail away – sail away.
When you feel your song is orchestrated wrong
Why should you prolong
Your stay?
When the wind and the weather blow your dreams sky
high
Sail away – sail away!

'Sail Away' from *Ace of Clubs* (1950)

⠿　　⠿　　⠿

When I'm feeling dreary and blue,
I'm only too
Glad to be left alone.
Dreaming of a place in the sun.
When day is done,
Far from a telephone . . .

I'm world weary, world weary,
Living in a great big town,
I find it so dreary, so dreary,
Everything looks grey or brown . . .

I can hardly wait
'Til I see the great
Open spaces,
My loving friends will not be there,
I'm so sick of their
God-damned faces.

'World Weary' from *This Year of Grace!* (1928)

⠿　　⠿　　⠿

I have always believed in putting geographical distance between myself and a flop.

Diaries (1948)

Much of his best work was done on the road to Samarkand (or somewhere similar).

> *I travel alone*
> *Sometimes I'm East,*
> *Sometimes I'm West,*
> *No chains can ever bind me;*
> *No remembered love can ever find me;*
> *I travel alone.*

'I Travel Alone' (1930)

The romantic in him liked to depict himself as the lone wanderer, the Flying (or Sailing) Englishman. The more mundane truth is that he rarely travelled alone but generally with one or more members of his loyal 'family'.

I love to go and I love to have been, but best of all I love the intervals between arrivals and departures.

Present Indicative (1937)

⁂   ⁂   ⁂

I love travelling, but I'm always too late or too early. I arrive in Japan when the cherry blossoms have fallen. I get to China too early for the next revolution. I reach Canada when the maple leaves have gone. People are always telling me about something I haven't seen. I find it very pleasant.

Diaries (1965)

⋮   ⋮   ⋮

Travel they say improves the mind,
An irritating platitude
Which frankly, entre nous,
Is very far from true . . .
There isn't a rock
Between Bangkok
And the beaches of Hispaniola,
That does not recoil
From suntan oil
And the gurgle of Coca-Cola

'Why do the Wrong People Travel?' from *Sail Away* (1961)

⋮   ⋮   ⋮

SEBASTIEN: And if you want a clear and concise
answer . . . about Americans being unpopular
abroad, I can give it to you now, firmly and
unequivocally. They take too many photographs
and ask too many questions.

Nude With Violin (1956)

⋮   ⋮   ⋮

In the course of my extensive wandering across the
world I have formed a strong aversion to tourists *en
masse* . . . I know that, ideally speaking, it is a 'good'
thing that people who have never set foot outside
their own back yards should be able to enjoy the
wonders of the world and I chide myself with fanciful
visions of sad little old ladies receiving unexpected
legacies and gallantly spending them on adventurous
travel. Unfortunately, however, very few of the old

ladies I have encountered on cruise ships have been either sad or little. On the contrary, most of them have been aggressive, full-bosomed, strident and altogether intolerable.

Past Conditional (1965)

⁂

There's nothing funnier than an Englishman travelling abroad.

Interview with Edgar Lustgarten (1972)

⁂

AMANDA: And India, the burning Ghars, or Ghats, or whatever they are, and the Taj Mahal. How *was* the Taj Mahal? . . . And it didn't look like a biscuit box, did it? I've always felt that it might.

Private Lives (1930)

⁂

I have not, as yet, seen the Taj Mahal at all, but I feel that when I do it will probably lie down in a consciously alluring attitude and pretend to be asleep.

Present Indicative (1937)

· 91 ·

⠿　⠿　⠿

I don't care for China,
Japan's far too small,
I've rumbled the Rio Grande,
I hate Asia Minor,
I can't bear Bengal
And I shudder to think
Of the awful stink
On the road to Samarkand.

'I Like America' from *Ace of Clubs* (1949)

Travelling certainly had its downside. Having slept uncomfortably in a hotel bed in the tropics, he was asked by the manager if the hotel could put up a sign to say 'Noël Coward Slept Here'. He replied:

If you'll add one word – 'Fitfully'.

⠿　⠿　⠿

I wonder who thought of introducing leatherette into the tropics? Whoever did should have his balls snipped off and fastened to his nose with a safety pin. This should also happen to whoever thought of leatherette in the first place.

Diaries (1968)

⠿　⠿　⠿

Sunburn is very becoming – but only when it is even. One must be careful not to look like a mixed grill.

'The Lido Beach' from *This Year of Grace!* (1928)

Reflecting on a 1944 African trip:

> The Dinkas' claim to fame is that they are very tall, have the longest penises in the world and dye their hair with urine; doubtless cause and effect.

Future Indefinite (1954)

⁜ ⁜ ⁜

BRIGHTEYES: No hard liquor before sundown. It's a rule I learned from the tropics.
IRENE: Which tropics?
BRIGHTEYES: Palm Beach.

Long Island Sound (1947)

⁜ ⁜ ⁜

As I mentioned this morning to Charlie,
There is far too much music in Bali,
And altho' as a place it's entrancing,
There is also a thought too much dancing . . .

And altho' all the 'lovelies' and 'Pretties'
Unblushingly brandish their titties,
The whole thing's a little too clever
And there's too much artistic endeavour!

Forgive the aforementioned Charlie,
I had to rhyme something with Bali.

'Bali', *Collected Verse* (1984)

Once again, the telegram provided a concise form of communication with his nearest and dearest:

HAVE MOVED HOTEL EXCELSIOR STOP COUGHING MYSELF INTO A FIRENZE

Telegram from Florence to Cole Lesley,
Remembered Laughter (1976)

On another occasion he wired:

AM BACK FROM ISTANBUL WHERE I WAS KNOWN AS ENGLISH DELIGHT.

Kenneth Tynan in *The New Yorker* (1977)

An ardent visitor, Coward was a less enthusiastic host. If a guest was welcome for a return engagement, he or she would be played out of the house with a recording of 'I'll See You Again'.

The most beautiful thing about having people to stay is when they leave.

Volcano (1957)

Exposure to a lifetime of travelling finally caused him to ask:

> *Why do the wrong people travel, travel, travel,*
> *When the right people stay back home?*
> *What explains this mass mania*
> *To leave Pennsylvania*
> *And clack around like flocks of geese,*
> *Demanding dry martinis on the Isles of Greece?*

'Why do the Wrong People Travel?' from *Sail Away* (1961)

On his travels Coward was increasingly appalled by the mind and manners of his fellow travellers. In *Suite in Three Keys* (1965), an American lady tourist is complaining to another about her husband's lack of enthusiasm for seeing the sights:

> I managed to drag him into Saint Peter's in Rome and all he did was stomp around humming 'I Like New York in June' under his breath. I was mortified.

And the final verdict on the world according to Coward?

> My body has certainly wandered a good deal, but I have an uneasy suspicion that my mind has not wandered nearly enough.

Present Indicative (1937)

:::   :::   :::

> *Free from love's illusion, my heart is my own –*
> *I travel alone.*

'I Travel Alone' (1930)

PART FIVE

::: ::: :::

'If Love Were All . . .'

Coward's image seemed to suggest that the brittle should predominate over the more sensitive emotions, yet, when asked for the one word which encapsulated his life, he was in no doubt. Nor did he seek to wrap it in an aphorism: 'LOVE'. Throughout his life he was alternately love's willing and unwilling victim, and he found that fame was no defence against its slings and arrows. He summed it up most personally, perhaps, through Manon, the cabaret singer:

> *I believe in doing what I can,*
> *In crying when I must,*
> *In laughing when I choose.*
> *Heigh-ho, if love were all*
> *I should be lonely . . .*
>
> *But I believe that since my life began*
> *The most I've had is just*
> *A talent to amuse*
> *Heigh-ho, if love were all!*

'If Love Were All' from *Bitter Sweet* (1929)

⁘　⁘　⁘

To love and be loved is the most important thing in the world but it is often painful.

(1950)

⁘　⁘　⁘

How idiotic people are when they're in love. What an age-old devastating disease.

Cole Lesley, *Remembered Laughter* (1976)

⁙   ⁙   ⁙

Cruelty, possessiveness and petty jealousy are traits you develop when in love.

⁙   ⁙   ⁙

To hell with God damned 'L'Amour'! It always causes far more trouble than it is worth. Don't run after it. Don't court it. Keep it waiting off stage until you're good and ready for it and even then treat it with the suspicious disdain that it deserves.

Letter to Marlene Dietrich (1956)

⁜   ⁜   ⁜

My private emotions are going through the usual
familiar hoops, hoops that I fondly imagined I had
discarded years ago. I am sure it is good for the soul
and the spirit and the ultimate creative processes to
fall down into the dust again, but it is now and always
has been painful for me. My extraordinary gift of
concentration, which stands me in such good stead in
all other phases of my life, turns on these occasions
into a double-edged sword. My imagination works
overtime and frequently inaccurately. I scale heights
and tumble down lachrymose ravines. My humour
retires baffled (but not for long, thank God), and I lie
awake arguing with myself, jeering at myself and,
worst of all, pitying myself. All the gallant lyrics of all
the songs I have ever written rise up and mock me
while I lie in the dark and listen. It all has little to do
with the person, little to do with anyone but myself.
To me, passionate love has been like a tight shoe
rubbing blisters on my Achilles heel. That's of that. I
resent it and love it and wallow and recover and it's all
part of 'life's rich pattern' and I wish to God I could
handle it, but I never have and now I never will.

(Oi, Oi, that's enough of that.)

Diaries (1957)

But Noel could be positive about the amorous emotion . . .

ELYOT: Love is no use unless it's wise, and kind, and
undramatic. Something steady and sweet, to
smooth out your nerves when you're tired.
Something tremendously cosy; and unflurried by

scenes and jealousies. That's what I want, what I've always wanted, really.

Private Lives (1930)

⁙　⁙　⁙

Love is a true understanding of just a few people for each other. Passionate love we will leave on one side for that rises, gets to its peak and dies away. True love is something much more akin to friendship and friendship, I suppose, is the greatest benison and compensation that Man has.

(1970)

Coward on love – and loss – is perhaps best expressed in his lyrics and verse, where the 'secret heart' can express itself without self-consciousness . . .

> *Tell me, what is love?*
> *Is it some consuming flame;*
> *Part of the moon, part of the sun,*
> *Part of a dream barely begun?*

'What Is Love?' from *Bitter Sweet* (1929)

⁙　⁙　⁙

> *Some day I'll find you,*
> *Moonlight behind you,*
> *True to the dream I am dreaming.*
> *As I draw near you*
> *You'll smile a little smile;*
> *For a little while*
> *We shall stand*
> *Hand in hand.*

'Some Day I'll Find You' from *Private Lives* (1930)

⠿ ⠿ ⠿

You were there
Your eyes looked into mine and faltered
Everywhere
The colour of the whole world altered
False became true,
My universe tumbled in two,
The earth became heaven, for you
Were there.

'You Were There' from 'Shadow Play'
from *Tonight At 8:30* (1936)

⠿ ⠿ ⠿

This is to let you know
That all that I feel for you
Can never wholly go.
I love you and miss you even two hours away,
With all my heart. This is to let you know.

'This is to Let You Know', *Collected Verse* (1984)

⠿ ⠿ ⠿

Let our affair be a gay thing
And when these hours have flown
Then, without forgetting
Happiness that has passed,
There'll be no regretting
Fun that didn't quite last . . .
Let's say, 'Goodbye' and leave it alone.

'Let's Say Goodbye' from *Words and Music* (1932)

⠿ ⠿ ⠿

Things can't last for ever,
Lover's hours are fleet,
Destiny may sever
Happiness complete,
Passion's so uncertain,
Some unfinished rhyme
May bring down the curtain
Long before it's time.

'The Dream Is Over' (1920s)

⠿　⠿　⠿

Do you remember those exquisite
Oysters we had in Peking?
And the stale caviar
That we ate in the bar
Of the Station Hotel in King's Lynn?
What a sophisticated pair
And what a dull love affair!

'The Parting of the Ways' from *Sigh No More* (1945)

⠿　⠿　⠿

Where are the songs we sung
When love in our hearts was young?
Where, in the limbo of the swiftly passing years,
Lie all our hopes and dreams and fears?
Where have they gone – words that rang so true
When Love in our hearts was new?

'Where are the Songs we Sung?'
from *Operette* (1938)

But then, there was love and there was marriage – an altogether more questionable enterprise. On that subject – never having tried it – Coward was (at least in print) of one mind:

OLIVE: Marriage nowadays is nothing but a temporary refuge for those who are uncomfortable at home.

The Rat Trap (1918)

⁙   ⁙   ⁙

RUTH: We've both been married before – careless rapture at this stage would be incongruous and embarrassing

Blithe Spirit (1941)

⁙   ⁙   ⁙

There are many reasons why you should marry – for love or for money – and many why you shouldn't.

⁙   ⁙   ⁙

Table d'hôte is marriage.
Free love is *à la carte*.

⁙   ⁙   ⁙

She married in haste and repented at Brixton.

Line of unused dialogue (c.1918)

⁙   ⁙   ⁙

ZOE: I must say I consider marriage an over-rated amusement.

This was a Man (1926)

⁜　⁜　⁜

TOBY: Marriage is a sacrament, a mystic rite, and you persist in regarding it as a sort of plumber's estimate.

'Ways and Means' from *Tonight At 8.30* (1935)

⁜　⁜　⁜

I consider boredom the most legitimate of all reasons for a divorce.

World Telegram (1931)

The simple fact of life for Coward was that men and women were two entirely different species, fundamentally incompatible and not meant to live together:

ELYOT: It doesn't suit women to be promiscuous.
AMANDA: It doesn't suit men for women to be promiscuous.

Private Lives (1930)

⁙   ⁙   ⁙

CICELY: Are you trying to drive me to my lover's arms?
GEORGE: I fail to see the point of driving you, dear, when you trot there so nicely by yourself.

The Young Idea (1922)

⁙   ⁙   ⁙

Why are men permitted to sin and sin again,
Say they're sorry and then begin again?
Have they certain glands that automatically combust?
Why is it accepted that they just must lust? . . .

Why are men acquitted of social treachery
When we women, with one light lechery,
Set our world ablaze?
Why is it the woman who pays and pays
To the end of her days?

'Why is it the Woman who Pays?'
from *After the Ball* (1954)

⁙   ⁙   ⁙

IRIS: I like men who go about a bit and see life.
LADY CARRINGTON: I suppose that's why so many
women marry commercial travellers.

The Unattainable (1918) – unproduced play

:::   :::   :::

– I don't think my husband's been entirely faithful
  to me.
– Whatever makes you think that?
– My last child doesn't resemble him in the slightest.

This Year of Grace! (1928)

Although he was perceptive in writing about women in his plays some of
his private musings would hardly have appealed to the Feminist Movement:

I can't think of one beautiful historical lady in a
position of power who wasn't a dithering idiot. I
suppose it's the beauty that does it. Oh, for the
humour and horse-sense of Queen Elizabeth I. I
have a feeling that Boadicea might have been fairly
bright but they were neither of them Gladys
Coopers.

(1969)

:::   :::   :::

Imagine the chaos that would ensue if our destinies
were ruled, even temporarily by Nancy Astor or
Clare Booth Luce! Beatrice Lillie would be
infinitely less perilous. Some day I must really
settle down to writing a biography of that arch-idiot
Joan of Arc.

Diaries (1967)

Beatrice Lille and Noël Coward

In his personal life Coward adored women and wrote most of his greatest parts for them.

> RUTH: Your view of women is academic to say the least of it – just because you've always been dominated by them it doesn't necessarily follow that you know anything about them.
>
> *Blithe Spirit* (1941)

Nonetheless, throughout his career they were perpetual targets of his pen. Noël's descriptions of women were not always of the most charitable . . .

> ELYOT: Certain women should be struck regularly, like gongs.
>
> *Private Lives* (1930)

⁙ ⁙ ⁙

I have drunk from the Well of Truth and I feel it incumbent upon me to say that no man could possibly go on loving you after he had seen you in curlers.

Line of unused dialogue (c. 1919)

⁙   ⁙   ⁙

LUELLA: Is it true that Winnie Schaeffer is going to have another baby?

LESTER: She can't be!

IRENE: Judging by the look of it she didn't *quite* have the last one.

Long Island Sound (1947)

⁙   ⁙   ⁙

SHOLTO: I don't think one *could* go too far with Priscilla. She has no distance.

The Young Idea (1921)

⁙   ⁙   ⁙

SANDRA: Poor Cuckoo . . . She's not bad once you get below the surface.

BOFFIN: I'll wear an aqua-lung.

South Sea Bubble (1956)

⁙   ⁙   ⁙

JUDITH: I detest her. She's far too old for you, and she goes about using Sex as a sort of shrimping-net.

Hay Fever (1924)

⁙   ⁙   ⁙

ERIC: I don't think women ought to go on being
vulnerable after forty. It diminishes them.

Star Quality (1967)

⋮   ⋮   ⋮

Her body had run to fat with such overdone
enthusiasm that she looked like an upholstered pear.

Beyond These Voices – unpublished novel

Not that male weakness fared any better:

> *Every peach out of reach is attractive*
> *'Cos it's just a little bit too high,*
> *And you'll find that every man*
> *Will try to pluck it if he can*
> *As he passes by.*
> *For the brute loves the fruit that's forbidden*
> *And I'll bet you half a crown*
> *He'll appreciate the flavour of it much, much more*
> *If he has to climb a bit to shake it down.*

'Forbidden Fruit' (1915)

True, the suggested wager of half a crown rather lets
down the tone. One cannot help feeling that a bet of
fifty pounds, or at least a fiver, would be more in
keeping with the general urbanity of the theme . . .
but this perhaps is hyper-criticism and it must also
be remembered that to the author half a crown in
1916 was the equivalent of five pounds in 1926. Also,
it rhymes with 'down'.

Present Indicative (1937)

Perhaps surprisingly, since he was homosexual, there are very few jokes at their expense – it was something he considered a personal matter. One of the few – probably because he found it impossible to pass up a good punch line – occurred when he visited Venice in 1936. Admiral of the Fleet, Sir Dudley Pound had arrived on his flagship. Pound and his wife decided to throw a party on board for the various celebrities who were in town and Noël and Lady Castlerosse were deputed to draw up the guest list. When they had done so, Lady Castlerosse looked at it dubiously and said to Noël:

'Noël, I have a dreadful feeling we've asked too many queer people.'

to which Noël replied:

'Don't worry. If we take care of the pansies, the Pounds will take care of themselves.'

⁛   ⁛   ⁛

Time and again
I'm tortured by contrition
And swear that I'm sorry I've sinned,
Then when I've lashed myself with whips and scourges
Sex emerges,
Out pop all the urges.

'Time and Again' (1955)

⁛   ⁛   ⁛

Sex and champagne as social institutions
Stampede me
And lead me astray

'Time and Again' (1966)

⁛   ⁛   ⁛

Freud could explain my curious condition
And Jung would have certainly grinned.
When I meet some sly dish
Who looks like my dish
I'm drunk – sunk – gone with the wind.

'Time and Again' (1955)

⁝　⁝　⁝

In cynical mood even sex was not all it was cracked up to be:

Sex and the weather have a good deal in common.

Observer (1969)

⁝　⁝　⁝

Travellers' cheques can
Do more than sex can . . .

'You're a Long, Long Way from America'
from *Sail Away* (1961)

Garry Essendine on sex:

To me the whole business is vastly over-rated. I
enjoy it for what it's worth and fully intend to go on
doing so for as long as anybody's interested and
when the time comes that they're not I shall be
perfectly content to settle down with an apple and a
good book!

Present Laughter (1939)

⁝　⁝　⁝

Pornography bores me, squalor disgusts me.

⠿   ⠿   ⠿

I think sex is over-rated practically everywhere – and sometimes under-rated. There is far too much nonsense talked about it.

(1969)

But sex could still be a source of amusement:

- A virgin bride shouldn't have the faintest idea what her husband looks like without his shirt.
- Bride I may be, but virgin comes under the heading of wishful thinking.
- I don't know what the younger generation is coming to.
- *I* do – and it's lovely.

'Bon Voyage'

⠿   ⠿   ⠿

SANDRA: Nothing has ever been able to convince the Samolans that sex is wrong. To them it's just as simple as eating mangoes.
BOFFIN: Only less stringy and indigestible.

South Sea Bubble (1956)

⠿   ⠿   ⠿

JUDY: You've no idea what you can have done to you nowadays, if you really put your mind to it. You can even have your sex changed at the drop of a hat.
NAOMI: King's Road, Chelsea must be knee deep in discarded bowlers.

Age Cannot Wither (1967) – unproduced play

Speaking more personally . . .

> I have enjoyed sex thoroughly, perhaps even
> excessively, all my life but it has never, except for
> brief wasteful moments, twisted my reason. I suspect
> that my sense of humour is as stubborn as my sanity,
> perhaps they're the same thing.

Letter to Edward Albee (1965)

:::   :::   :::

And yet in his more realistic moments he could admit that his emotional
judgements were often flawed . . .

> . . . something that I didn't myself realise at the time
> . . . was that apart from the swans which really were
> swans, I had a dangerous capacity for seeing nearly
> all geese as those beautiful birds: dangerous for me,
> that is – the geese naturally enjoyed it enormously . . .
> perhaps I have wasted too much time before realising
> that a number of them were not even geese but only
> lame ducks . . .
>
> There is a whole universe of difference between
> discovering and encouraging hidden capabilities in
> other people and over-estimating non-existent ones
> . . . Alas, it is a mistake we often make, especially
> when looking through eyes misting with love, that
> notorious impairer of hitherto perfect vision. Then,
> with our eyesight still off-true and rose-coloured, we
> heave the loved one on to a pedestal, an insecure
> lodging at best, and are unreasonably embittered and
> discouraged if the loved one should totter and fall.
> No, no – never demand from people more than they
> are capable of giving.

'The Best Advice I Ever Had' – Reader's Digest (1958)

As far as his own contribution to the Battle of the Sexes was concerned:

> I am the world's sexiest man . . . Indeed, if I put my mind to it, I am sure I could pass the supreme test and lure Miss Taylor away from Mr. Burton.
>
> Dick Richards, *The Wit of Noël Coward* (1968)

Noël was once being conducted around the red-light district of Honolulu:

> . . . when to my great surprise from an upstairs room in a down-at-the-heel bordello I heard the sound of my own voice singing – 'London Pride has been handed down to us . . .' I didn't think I'd be all that much of a come-on – but apparently I am!
>
> Television interview with David Frost (1969)

But – as was so often the case – the deeper feelings were left to the privacy of verse:

> *Time and tide can never sever*
> *Those whom love has bound forever.*
>
> 'Lover Of My Dreams' from *Cavalcade* (1931)

⁘　⁘　⁘

> *I am no good at love*
> *I betray it with little sins*
> *For I feel the misery of the end*
> *In the moment that it begins*
> *And the bitterness of the last good-bye*
> *Is the bitterness that wins.*
>
> 'I am No Good at Love' from *Not Yet the Dodo* (1967)

⁘　⁘　⁘

There's no more to say about love,
The poets have said it for ages,
They rhyme it with 'dove' and
    'above'
And praise it for pages and pages,
There isn't one passionate phrase
    that they miss,
Yet lovers find new ones each time
    that they kiss.
So what's a love poet to do
When lovers are all poets too?

'There's No More To Say About Love' (c.1937) –
unpublished song

PART SIX

⣿ ⣿ ⣿

'Sigh No More'

Oh, God!

That remark no longer has any dramatic significance. One uses it when one can't find a taxi!

⁛   ⁛   ⁛

My mind is . . . not really attuned to the Church of England or any other church for that matter. I loathe all that insistence on being a miserable sinner and asking for forgiveness. The traditional part of it is all right with the squeaky hymns and the choir (mixed) and the best bibs and tuckers and all the age-old carry-on, but the fundamental faith underlying it is missing in me. I never have felt and don't feel now the call of the Holy Spirit, and I suspect I never shall.

Diaries (1964)

Many people are surprised to find that religion – however disorganised – was a thread that ran through Coward's life. His attitude to it was at best ambivalent but, like a spiritual itch, he kept scratching it:

> *Do I believe in God?*
> *Well, yes, I suppose in a sort of way*
> *It's really terribly hard to say.*
>
> 'Do I Believe?' from *Collected Verse* (1984)

⁛   ⁛   ⁛

· 121 ·

If I should ultimately meet my God,
He will not be the God of love or Battles,
He'll be some under God whose job it is
To organise sharp sounds and things that rattle.
He'll be the one who, all my life on earth,
Can, most sadistically, my spirit shatter
With little hammerings and sudden shouts
And hollow ricochets of empty mirth.

'Lines to God' – unpublished verse

His first exposure was early. As a nine-year-old child performer he was asked to sing anthems in churches:

But I hated doing this because the lack of applause depressed me. It irritated me when I had soared magnificently through 'God is a Spirit' or 'Oh, For the Wings of a Dove' to see the entire congregation scuffle on to their knees murmuring gloomy 'Amens' instead of clapping loudly and shouting 'Bravo'.

Present Indicative (1937)

⁞   ⁞   ⁞

I had a religious mania lasting exactly one day and based on an inexplicable fear of death which descended upon me abruptly in the middle of a matinée . . . There was thunder in the air as well, and during that night a terrific storm broke, convincing me that this was my destined finish. I wept thoroughly at the vivid picture of Mother's face when she heard how the sharp lightning had struck her darling through the window of the second floor back. I murmured incoherent prayers, vowed many vows

and promised many promises, if only I might live a
little longer. They were apparently granted, for I
woke up the next morning as bright as a button and
rapidly forgot the whole episode, promises and all.

(c. 1916)

At sixteen the contact with religion was rather more personal. In a 1969
television interview he told David Frost how at his Confirmation class the
local vicar had touched his knee, causing Coward to remark:

Vicar, you are supposed to be preparing me for
Confirmation. When I have received the gift of the
Holy Spirit, if I'm in the mood, I'll telephone you.

Nor was this to be his only brush with the Church (so to speak). When the
local vicar called at his Kent home early in 1946:

He talked a great deal of cock and never drew breath.
Matelot (Coward's dog) complicated the interview by
attempting to rape him. I removed him saying –
'Matelot, *not* the vicar!'

Diaries (1946)

Although he could reflect on God in the privacy of his *Diaries* or in verse,
he became self-conscious when the subject cropped up in public. In the
interview with Frost he was asked about his attitude to God:

We've never been intimate – but maybe we do have a
few things in common.

. . . and when Frost pressed him on his personal visions of Hell:

They're all to do with over-acting!

(1969)

Nor was he averse to invoking the Deity on really important occasions. For instance, the afternoon nap was sacrosanct. He told Cole Lesley, his chief aide:

> If God rings, tell Him I'm not in.
>
> Cole Lesley, *Remembered Laughter* (1976)

⁝   ⁝   ⁝

LEO: Doesn't the Eye of Heaven mean anything to you?

GILDA: Only when it winks!

> *Design For Living* (1932)

⁝   ⁝   ⁝

LADY CARRINGTON: Prayer only becomes really
trying when one has linoleum in one's bedroom.

The Unattainable (1918) – unpublished play

⁂   ⁂   ⁂

She surveyed the house with a bright smile, the sort
of smile you receive from a Christian Scientist when
you announce that you have a toothache.

Beyond These Voices – unpublished novel

⁂   ⁂   ⁂

I don't know who it was who said, 'The only time I
believe in God is when I write', but whoever it was
said a mouthful.

Diaries (1955)

⁂   ⁂   ⁂

I have little reverence for the teachings of Christian
Science; as a religion it has always seemed to me to
induce a certain air of superiority in its devotees, as
well as encouraging them to swish their skirts aside
from many of life's unspiritual, but quite
unquestionable, realities.

Future Indefinite (1954)

⁂   ⁂   ⁂

Christianity has caused a great deal more suffering
both mentally and physically, than any other religion
in the history of mankind . . . the endless succession
of tortured, oppressed, Puritan-ridden generations

that have resulted from that unfortunately over-publicised episode at Jerusalem 1,995 years ago. I must say it is a little hard on Jesus Christ to be for ever associated with such a monumental balls-up

Diaries (1955)

⁂   ⁂   ⁂

GRIZEL: God moves in mysterious ways.

LUCY: That sounds blasphemous.

GRIZEL: Nature, then. Almost every natural instinct we have leads us straight as a die to the most appalling indignities. I expect that's why all those dreary religious reformers carry on the way they do about sex being a sin and the life of the spirit being the thing to hang on to tooth and claw. They must be mortified every time they go to the loo.

Pomp and Circumstance (1960) – play version

⁂   ⁂   ⁂

ELYOT: All the futile moralists who try to make life unbearable. Laugh at them. Be flippant. Laugh at everything, all their sacred shibboleths. Flippancy brings out the acid in their damned sweetness and light . . .

Let's be superficial and pity the poor Philosophers. Let's blow trumpets and squeakers, and enjoy the party as much as we can, like very small, quite idiotic school-children.

Private Lives (1930)

⁂   ⁂   ⁂

You'll grow out of it, dear, it's only a passing phase like thrush or measles. Girls always begin with religious mania, then become atheists and after that agnostics. When these three milestones are past, one can comfortably expect to settle down.

Line of unused dialogue (c. 1918)

⁜ ⁜ ⁜

I happen to love life as it is and not as it should be and I can envisage no steady reforms of the human spirit and if, by some magic, everybody became spiritually impeccable, I am quite convinced that they would bore the b'Jesus out of me.

Letter to Esmé Wynne-Tyson (1952)

⁜ ⁜ ⁜

I knew, in my teens, that the world was full of hatred, envy, malice, cruelty, jealousy, unrequited love, murder, despair and destruction. I also knew, at the same time, that it was full of kindness, joy, pleasure, requited love, generosity, fun, excitement, laughter and friends. Nothing that has happened to me over the years has caused me to re-adjust in my mind the balance of those observed phenomena.

Diaries

In his writings – often through the mouths of his characters – he would speculate on the Great Mysteries of the Universe:

CHARLES: Life without faith is an arid business.

Blithe Spirit (1941)

⁙ ⁙ ⁙

LEO: Life is a pleasure trip
. . . a Cheap Excursion.

Design For Living (1932)

⁙ ⁙ ⁙

Life is nothing but a game
of make-believe –

'When My Ship Comes Home'
from *London Calling* (1923)

⁙ ⁙ ⁙

MADAME ARCATI: Time is
the reef upon which all our
frail mystic ships are
wrecked.

Blithe Spirit (1941)

⁙ ⁙ ⁙

'Morality' was not the word that leapt immediately to mind in conversations about Coward and yet he wrote *The Vortex*, he said, out of a 'moral impetus'. So what, asked David Frost, do you do with your moral impetus nowadays?

I give it a little groundsel and feed it gently – it does
all right.

Television interview (1970)

⁙ ⁙ ⁙

Astrology. I wasn't passionately interested in whether I was a Sagittarius or Taurus. I thought I was just *me*. Which is a very Sagittarian thing to say.

⁝   ⁝   ⁝

LOUISE: Life is awfully funny, isn't it?
EVAN: Not monotonously so.

Long Island Sound (1947)

⁝   ⁝   ⁝

CLINTON: I believe that life is for living, don't you?
SEBASTIEN: It's difficult to know what else one could do with it.

Nude With Violin (1956)

⁝   ⁝   ⁝

Tout lasse, tout passe, tout casse. Life goes on and little bits of us get lost.

Diaries (1957)

Noël is here misquoting from Charles Cahier's *Quelque six mille proverbes* (1856) – No. 1718. It had long been a favourite of his but what he *should* have written was '*Tout passe, tout casse, tout lasse*' ('Everything passes, everything perishes, everything palls.')

⁝   ⁝   ⁝

The world to me will always be a gamble,
I don't care if I win or if I lose.

'Cosmopolitan Lady' from *On With the Dance* (1925)

⠿　⠿　⠿

Time, as I have so often wittily said, is a great healer.

Diaries (1963)

And as for humankind . . .

The human race is cruel, idiotic, sentimental,
predatory, ungrateful, ugly, conceited and egocentric
to the last ditch and the occasional discovery of an
isolated exception is as deliciously surprising as
finding a sudden Brazil nut in what you *know* to be
five pounds of vanilla creams.

⠿　⠿　⠿

I care a very great deal about the human race; it is,
when all is said and done, all we have got.

Dick Richards, *The Wit of Noël Coward* (1968)

⠿　⠿　⠿

I have no deep thoughts about the human race, nor am
I particularly interested in reforming it; indeed, if I
did, there would be nothing left for me to write about.

⠿　⠿　⠿

ISOBEL: Just fancy! One lives and learns, doesn't one?
SEBASTIEN: That's certainly one of the more
prevalent human illusions, madame.

Nude With Violin (1956)

⠿　⠿　⠿

COLEY: Well, we live and learn, don't we?
NOËL: Yes, and we die and forget it all

Cole Lesley,
Remembered Laughter (1976)

⁖   ⁖   ⁖

Cole [Lesley] and I had a long and cosy talk
about death the other evening . . . we came to the
sensible conclusion that there was nothing to be
done. We should have to get on with life until our
time came. I said, 'After all, the day had to go on
and breakfast had to be eaten', and he replied that
if I died he might find it a little difficult to eat
breakfast but would probably be peckish by
lunch-time.

Diaries (1961)

⁖   ⁖   ⁖

ELYOT: Death's very laughable, such a cunning little
mystery. All done with mirrors.

Private Lives (1930)

⁖   ⁖   ⁖

The finality of death is bewildering on first
acquaintance and the words 'never again' too sad to
believe entirely.

Present Indicative (1937)

⁖   ⁖   ⁖

How little they had to fear, those Victorians,
compared with us . . . The idea of death had so much
more dignity and grace. Lovesick girls went into
'declines' and had a little calf's-foot jelly and expired;
poets coughed their lives away in sanatoriums and
died peacefully, murmuring lovely things to their
loved ones.

'This Time Tomorrow'

∷　∷　∷

Death seems to me as natural a process as birth;
inevitable, absolute and final. If, when it happens to
me, I find myself in a sort of Odeon ante-room
queuing up for an interview with Our Lord, I shall
be very surprised indeed.

Diaries (1955)

At the end of the war the authorities came across the Nazi list of people to
be liquidated immediately Britain was occupied. Sharing top billing were
Noël and his friend, Rebecca West, who sent him a post-card . . .

MY DEAR, THE PEOPLE WE SHOULD HAVE
BEEN SEEN DEAD WITH.

The young Coward must have felt himself to be immortal but, as with
everyone, the passing years took their toll, and age became a recurrent
topic:

Time's wingèd chariot is beginning to goose me.

Diaries (1959)

∷　∷　∷

How do you do, middle age?
Autumn winds begin to blow
And so
I'd better unbend my mind to you
Though you know
I'm not quite yet resigned to you,
More relaxation,
More ease,
More time for snoozing,
What consolation
Are these
For those amusing
Pleasures I'm losing?
Shall I survive this decade
Or shall I merely fade out,
Done for – played out?
What are your designs for the final page?

'Middle Age' from *The Girl Who Came To Supper* (1963)

⁂ ⁂ ⁂

It is said that old age has its compensations. I wonder what they are?

Diaries (1967)

::: ::: :::

MAUDIE: Who was it that said there was something beautiful about growing old?

BONITA: Whoever it was, I have news for him.

Waiting in the Wings (1960)

::: ::: :::

PAWNIE: I expect Florence will just go on and on, then suddenly become quite beautifully old and go on and on still more.

HELEN: It's too late for her to become beautifully old, I'm afraid. She'll have to be young indefinitely.

The Vortex (1924)

::: ::: :::

> *Advancing years may bring about*
> *A rather sweet nostalgia*
> *In spite of rheumatism and gout*
> *And, certainly, neuralgia.*

'Something on a Tray' from *After the Ball* (1954)

::: ::: :::

One of the pleasures of growing older is the realisation that to be alone does not necessarily imply loneliness. For many years it has been my habit wherever I may be, to take an evening off, to relax my nerves, to gaze objectively at the world about me and the world within me; to know, for a few brief hours, that no contribution is required of me, neither wit, wisdom, sparkling repartee nor sage advice. On these quiet occasions I am always stimulated by the feeling that adventure may be just around the corner; not adventure in the sexual or dramatic sense, but adventure of the mind; something to distract, an idea, a sudden flick of memory, an observed incident, trivial in itself perhaps, but sharp and clear enough to quicken my creative impulse and fire my imagination.

Beyond These Voices – unpublished novel

⁙   ⁙   ⁙

His advice to Edith Evans:

If a person over fifty tries too hard to be 'with it', they soon find they're without everything.

Attributed

⁙   ⁙   ⁙

I have never felt the necessity of being 'with it'. I'm all for staying in my place.

John Lahr, *Coward the Playwright* (1982)

⁙   ⁙   ⁙

Age is very curious. You must accept it yet ignore it at the same time. You should never try to be younger than you are.

Interview with Hunter Davies (1969)

⋮ ⋮ ⋮

HELEN: You're ten years older than I am, but when I'm your age I shall be twenty years older than you.
FLORENCE: *Darling,* how deliciously involved – what *can* you mean by that?

The Vortex (1924)

Trying to talk to Marlene Dietrich on the subject of old age:

I said to her, with an effort at grey comedy, 'All I demand from my friends nowadays is that they live through lunch', to which she replied, puzzled, 'Why *lunch*, sweetheart?'

Diaries (1968)

Caricature by William Auerbach-Levy

A few years earlier he had tried the line out on actress Benita Hume. At that point the meal of choice had been 'dinner'. Presumably, in refining it, he decided 'lunch' had a greater poignancy.

On his 69th birthday:

> I sat up in bed submerged in [gift] wrappings and looking like an ancient Buddhist priest with a minor attack of jaundice. One year off seventy now! Just fancy. The snows of yesteryear are a bloody long way off.
>
> *Diaries* (1968)

⁛　⁛　⁛

> Old age is cruel and death much kinder when it is gentle.
>
> *Diaries* (1953)

⁛　⁛　⁛

> Personally I wish only for ultimate oblivion, which is fortunate because I think it is all I shall get . . . Why not get on with the material and experience at hand and try to make the best of it? . . . I am neither impressed by, nor frightened of, death. I admit that I am scared about the manner of my dying.
>
> *Diaries* (1955)

⁛　⁛　⁛

Personally I would rather not wait until the faculties begin to go. However, that must be left in the hands of 'The One Above' and I hope he'll do something about it and not just sit there.

Diaries (1965)

⁙   ⁙   ⁙

I would prefer Fate to allow me to go to sleep when it's my proper bedtime. I never have been one for staying up too late.

Diaries (1967)

⁙   ⁙   ⁙

I'll settle without apprehension for oblivion. I cannot really feel that oblivion will be disappointing. Life and love and fame and fortune can all be disappointing, but not dear old oblivion. Hurray for eternity.

Diaries (1961)

Nonetheless, he did find compensations in the love of 'family' and friends:

> *When I have fears, as Keats had fears,*
> *Of the moment I'll cease to be*
> *I console myself with vanished years*
> *Remembered laughter, remembered tears,*
> *And the peace of the changing sea.*

Collected Verse (1984)

⁙   ⁙   ⁙

As one gets older people begin to die and when each
one goes a little light goes out.

Diaries (1949)

⁙   ⁙   ⁙

The Grim Reaper has been at it again . . . One by one
they go – a bit chipped off here, a bit chipped off
there. It is an inevitability that one must prepare the
heart and mind for . . . Those I have really loved are
with me in moments of memory – whole and intact
and unchanged. I cannot envisage them in another
sphere. I do not even wish to.

Diaries (1961)

⁙   ⁙   ⁙

I can enjoy retrospective laughter again and again,
but retrospective tears never. The eyes remain dry.

⁙   ⁙   ⁙

We shall still be together
When our life's journey ends,
For wherever we chance to go
We shall always be friends.
We may find while we're travelling through the years
Moments of joy and love and happiness.
Reason for grief, reason for tears.
Come the wild, wild weather,
If we've lost or we've won,
We'll remember these words we say
Till our story is done.

'Come the Wild, Wild Weather' (1960)

⸬   ⸬   ⸬

There is no sense in grief, it wastes emotional energy.

Diaries (1967)

⸬   ⸬   ⸬

I do not approve of mourning, I approve only of remembering!

But even so. . .

It is a natural enough malaise, this idealised remembering, but should not be encouraged too much. There is no future in the past.

Diaries

Noël died peacefully in Jamaica at the age of 73.

PART SEVEN

⁙ ⁙ ⁙

Envoi:
'I'll See You Again'

Coward's best invention was himself. As the years went by he got into the habit of reviewing himself as though he were a character in one of his own plays – and, indeed, without too much of a stretch, he is to be found lurking inside certain of them. Garry Essendine in *Present Laughter* (1939) is perhaps the most obvious, and demonstrates the apparent paradox between the shy man and the show-off:

> GARRY: I don't give a hoot about posterity. Why should I worry about what people think of me when I'm dead as a doornail anyway? My worst defect is that I am apt to worry too much about what people think of me when I'm alive.
>
> *Present Laughter* (1939)

Looking back on his life Coward could conclude:

> First I was the *enfant terrible*. Then the Bright Young
> Thing. Now I'm a tradition.

Humble origins were most definitely de rigeur as the basis for a dramatic
life:

> I was truculent apparently about being born and
> made, with my usual theatrical acumen, a delayed
> entrance.

Diaries (1954)

⁑ ⁑ ⁑

> Oh, how fortunate I was to be born poor. If mother
> had been able to afford to send me to private school,
> Eton and Oxford or Cambridge, it would probably
> have set me back years.

Diaries (1967)

⁑ ⁑ ⁑

> My good fortune was to have a bright, acquisitive,
> but not, *not* an intellectual mind, and to have been
> impelled by circumstances to get out and earn my
> living and help with the instalments on the house.

Diaries (1969)

⁑ ⁑ ⁑

I have always distrusted too much education and intellectualism; it seems to me that they are always dead wrong about things that really matter.

Diaries (1967)

After a nervous breakdown in the early 1920s his doctor advised Noël to sit down and conduct an honest self-analysis of his strengths and weaknesses. He did so and called it a 'Mental Purge' . . .

DEFECTS

Over emotional and hysterical

Over anxiety to attain popularity

Jealousy fostered by over introspection

Intolerance

Lack of restraint – particularly emotionally

Self pitying

Predatory

Sentimental

Almost complete ignorance upon many subjects that I should know thoroughly, and a facility for faking knowledge

Physical cowardice

Histrionic in private life

Given to mental gymnastics at cost of other people's peace of mind

Domineering

Over emphatic in argument and practically everything

ASSETS

An excellent knowledge of psychology when
   unaffected by emotion

Strong sense of humour

Facility in conversation

Power of demanding and holding affection

Loyalty to friends and personal standards

Generosity and kindness of heart

Power of concentration

Several talents

Moral courage

Strength of will when unaffected by emotion

Common sense

Personality

⁂   ⁂   ⁂

If I'm in a group of people who are talking about
high policies, I have sense enough to keep quiet and
listen to them. And if they happen to be talking about
finance, I keep much quieter and possibly go to sleep.

Evening Standard (1966)

⁂   ⁂   ⁂

I was never, never in my life shy.

The Times (1969)

As it was he gave the journalists a helping hand in the shaping of the
appropriate persona, and charted not only where he intended to go but
also how to get there.

I am determined to travel through life first class.

Dick Richards, The Wit of Noël Coward (1968)

⁂ ⁂ ⁂

I am related to no one except myself.

Press conference (1920)

⁂ ⁂ ⁂

I've got an unworthy passion for popularity.

Easy Virtue (1923)

⁂ ⁂ ⁂

I have always prided myself on my capacity for being just one jump ahead of what everybody expects of me.

. . . and if the jump didn't always succeed . . .

We must press on and rise above it.

He was also fond of quoting Milton's *Lycidas* . . .

> *At last he rose, and twitched his mantle blue;*
> *Tomorrow to fresh woods and pastures new.*

When his own career 'song' seemed to be 'orchestrated wrong' he confided to Cole Lesley:

I shall always pop out of another hole in the ground. I shall twitch my mantle blue, tomorrow to fresh woods and pastures new. Oh, I do wish people wouldn't always misquote that line [as 'fresh fields'].

⁛　⁛　⁛

If I don't care for things I simply don't look at them.

Dick Richards, *The Wit of Noël Coward* (1968)

And over the years there were a number of things he didn't much care for . . .

Most of my gift horses seem to have come with very bad teeth.

Present Indicative (1937)

⁛　⁛　⁛

I believe whole-heartedly in pleasure. As much pleasure as possible and as much work. I am very light-minded and very serious. I have no religion, but I believe in courage. I loathe fear and cruelty and hatred and destructiveness . . .

Daily Mail (1962)

Every now and again along the way the self-seeker stops to take stock:

SHE: I've over-educated myself in all the things I shouldn't have known at all.

Mild Oats (1922)

⁛　⁛　⁛

My sense of my importance to the world is relatively small. On the other hand, my sense of my own importance to myself is tremendous.

Present Indicative (1937)

Fame when it came was instant.

> Success took me to her bosom like a maternal boa
> constrictor.
>
> *A Talent to Amuse* (1969)

And since it came with *The Vortex* (1924), in which Coward played a young drug addict, the popular image was ready made and the 'effete young man' was happy to humour the Press:

> I really have a frightfully depraved mind. I am never
> out of opium dens, cocaine dens and other evil places.
> My mind is a mass of corruption.

Commenting (ironically!) to the *Evening Standard* on the press speculation caused by the opening of the play:

> No Press interviewer, photographer, or gossip-writer
> had to fight in order to see me, I was wide open to
> them all, smiling and burbling bright witticisms,
> giving my views on this and that, discussing such
> problems as whether or not the modern girl would
> make a good mother. I was photographed in every
> conceivable position . . . the legend of my modesty
> grew. I became extraordinarily unspoiled by my great
> success. As a matter of fact, I still am.
>
> *Present Indicative* (1937)

:::   :::   :::

It's inevitable that the more successful I become, the
more people will run after me. I don't believe in their
friendship, and I don't take them seriously, but I
enjoy them. Probably a damn sight more than they

enjoy me! I enjoy the whole damned thing. I've worked hard for it all my life. They'll drop me, all right, when they're tired of me.

> The prophetic words of Leo – the character Noël played
> in *Design For Living* (1932)

Whatever the subject, an interviewer could be sure of a quotable answer. His idea of a perfect meal?

A little smoked salmon, a medium steak and perhaps some onions and chocolate ice cream. I've always been queer for chocolate!

His idea of comfort?

Good books, agreeable people and first-rate plumbing.

> Ed Murrow's *Small World* (1956)

The fact that he became a skilled subject for an interview never changed the fact that he was deeply suspicious of the Press as an institution . . .

Let's fly away
To where no threats of war obsess us
And where the Press does not depress us
Every single day . . .

I frankly say
I tear up each paper that publicises
The rather uninspiring enterprises
Of truck-drivers' wives who win competitions
By photographing birds in odd positions,
I don't care if a widow in Thames Ditton
Plunged into a well to save her kitten.

> 'Let's Fly Away' – adaptation of 1930 Cole Porter song

Was there anything he could *not* do?

> I could not dance in my own ballet.

On another occasion he would paraphrase . . .

> Well, I still can't saw ladies in half, or perform on the
> trapeze; but I'm working on it.
>
> Dick Richards, *The Wit of Noël Coward* (1968)

The unqualified success of the early 1920s was, in many ways, both the best
and the worst thing that happened to him. The eventual dilution of it
certainly brought perspective.

> GILDA: Success is far more perilous than failure,
> isn't it?
>
> *Design For Living* (1932)

Though the fame would continue unabated, the acclaim would never reach
the same decibel level as before, and for much of the rest of his life Coward
would gently mock his own image:

> In those days I was considered daring – now I'm
> practically Louisa M. Alcott.
>
> (1970)

There were occasional surrealistic moments when Fame seemed prepared
to desert him entirely . . .

> The only bright moment in the hospital was when a
> perfectly strange lady with orange hair bounced into
> my room and said – 'Are you Miss Davis and would
> you like a shampoo?' I replied coldly in the negative
> to both questions.
>
> *Diaries* (1964)

Asked by luncheon guest, Beverley Baxter whether he had survived the war, he assured him that he most certainly had. On relating the conversation later, he told Cole Lesley:

Like Mother Goddam, I shall always survive.

(1946)

⁙　　⁙　　⁙

My face is not my fortune but it must be watched, if only for professional reasons. It is now all right and the correct shape, but it is no longer a young face and if it were it would be macabre. It is strange to examine it carefully and compare it with early photographs.

Diaries (1956)

He had very little patience with the would-be *enfants terribles* treading so rudely on his heels. In a 1932 song he could write that 'there's a younger Generation knock, knock, knocking at the door'. But now:

[I] cannot understand why the younger generation, instead of knocking at the door, should bash the fuck out of it.

Diaries (1957)

⁙　　⁙　　⁙

I like being chic. The young enchanters of today may have talent but why must they look so grubby? I think you should always look your best. I know it's not important but it's silly to be deliberately grubby. I've always had a feeling for being an attractive public figure. I would do nothing to spoil it.

Interview with Hunter Davies (1969)

During the late fifties and early sixties he was the target of much media browbeating – all of which he managed to rise above:

> It has been most gratifying . . . I now find myself as big a celebrity as Debbie Reynolds.
>
> Dick Richards, *The Wit of Noël Coward* (1968)

In this he was again recycling himself. In 1946 it had been 'Stalin and James Mason' – *Diaries* (1946).

> The only thing that intrigues me is that at the age of 56 I can still command such general abuse.
>
> Interview (1956)

☷ ☷ ☷

> The battle, of course, will never end until the grave closes over me and then, oh dear, the balls that will be written about me.
>
> *Diaries* (1964)

☷ ☷ ☷

> Whenever I reflect with what alarming rapidity I am trundling towards old age and the dusty grave, I find it comforting to count my blessings. And although the future, like the late Mrs. Fiske, is heavily veiled, my blessings, up to date, have certainly been considerable.
>
> *Past Conditional* (1965)

☷ ☷ ☷

I'm not particularly interested in being remembered.
It would be nice to have a little niche in posterity but
it's not one of those dreadful things that haunts me.

⁑   ⁑   ⁑

> *I'm here for a short visit only*
> *And I'd rather be loved than hated*
> *Eternity may be lonely*
> *When my body's disintegrated*
> *And that which is loosely called my soul*
> *Goes whizzing off through the infinite*
> *By means of some vague, remote control*
> *I'd like to think I was missed a bit.*

'I'm Here for a Short Visit Only',
Collected Verse (1984)

Through it all he kept faith with himself:

The Almighty may write me out but I shall not write
myself out.

Sunday Express (1963)

⁑   ⁑   ⁑

I'm an enormously talented man, and there's no use
pretending I'm not.

Sunday Express (1965)

⁑   ⁑   ⁑

I think on the whole I am a better writer than I am given credit for being. It is fairly natural that my writing should be appreciated casually, because my personality, performances, music and legend get in the way. Someday I suspect, when Jesus has definitely got me for a sunbeam, my works may be adequately assessed.

Diaries (1956)

⁙   ⁙   ⁙

Really, my life has been one long extravaganza.

On re-reading his journals

Coward enjoyed the rewards success had brought him:

The world has treated me very well – but then I haven't treated it so badly either.

Ed Murrow's *Small World* (1959)

⁙   ⁙   ⁙

The public are very fond of me. I've done well by them, given them a lot. I'm proud that I'm popular and I've tried my best not to spoil it.

New York Times (1969)

⁙   ⁙   ⁙

I've had a wonderful life. I've still got rhythm, I've got music, who could ask for anything more?

Diaries (1961)

When his reputation was re-established in the mid-1960s, in what he gleefully dubbed 'Dad's Renaissance', he accepted victory with the same insouciance as he had embraced defeat. On the *Dick Cavett Show* (1970) the normally imperturbable Cavett was clearly tongue-tied in the presence of the abnormally imperturbable Noël:

CAVETT: You're – you . . . what is the word when one has such terrific, prolific qualities?

NOËL: Talent.

When the belated knighthood finally arrived, the investiture had an unintended touch of theatre that was not lost on the about-to-be Sir Noël.

As I advanced the music changed from 'Hello, Dolly' to 'A Life On the Ocean Wave'.

Letter to Nancy Mitford (1970)

My philosophy is as simple as ever – smoking, drinking, moderate sexual intercourse on a diminishing scale, reading and writing (not arithmetic). I have a selfish absorption in the well-being and achievement of Noël Coward.

Television interview (1970)

To what did he attribute his longevity?

To constant smoking and marrons glacés.

⁙ ⁙ ⁙

What – he was asked on his seventieth birthday – would he like as his epitaph?

He was much loved because he made people laugh and cry.

What were the two most beautiful things in the world?

Peace of mind and a sense of humour.

And how would he wish to be remembered?

By my charm.

His greatest single regret?

Not having taken more trouble with some of my work.

What was his idea of a perfect life?

Mine.

⁜　⁜　⁜

There will be lists of apocryphal jokes I never made
and gleeful misquotations of words I never said.
What a pity I shan't be here to enjoy them!

Diaries (1955)

⁘　⁘　⁘

With my usual watchful eye on posterity, I can only suggest to any wretched future biographer that he gets my daily engagement book and from that fills in anything he can find and good luck to him, poor bugger.

Diaries (1969)

⁘　⁘　⁘

My life has left me with no persistent regrets of any kind. I don't look back in anger, nor in anything approaching even mild rage; I rather look back in pleasure and amazement and amusement at the way my life has gone. It really has all been most enjoyable.

In a late TV interview he was asked to sum his life up in a single word. After an uncharacteristically long pause, he replied . . .

Well, now comes the terrible decision as to whether to be corny or not.

The answer *is* one word. Love.

To know that you are among people you love and who love you. That has made all the successes wonderful – much more wonderful than they'd have been anyway.

And that's it, really . . .

SAVING YOUR SECOND MARRIAGE BEFORE IT STARTS

WORKBOOK FOR MEN

RESOURCES BY LES AND LESLIE PARROTT

3 Seconds (by Les)

The Complete Guide to Marriage Mentoring (and workbooks and video)

The Control Freak (by Les)

Crazy Good Sex (by Les)

Dot.com Dating

The First Drop of Rain (by Leslie)

Getting Ready for the Wedding

God Loves You Nose to Toes (children's book by Leslie)

The Good Fight

Helping Your Struggling Teenager (by Les)

High Maintenance Relationships (by Les)

The Hour That Matters Most

I Love You More (and workbooks and video)

L.O.V.E.

The Love List

Love Talk (and workbooks and video)

Love Talk Devotional

Making Happy

Meditations on Proverbs for Couples

The Parent You Want to Be

Questions Couples Ask

Real Relationships (and workbook and video)

Saving Your Marriage Before It Starts (and workbooks and video)

Saving Your Second Marriage Before It Starts (and workbooks and video)

Seven Secrets of a Healthy Dating Relationship (by Les)

Soul Friends (by Leslie)

Trading Places (and workbooks)

You Matter More Than You Think (by Leslie)

You're Stronger Than You Think (by Les)

Your Time-Starved Marriage (and workbooks and video)

SAVING YOUR SECOND MARRIAGE BEFORE IT STARTS

WORKBOOK FOR MEN

*Nine Questions to Ask Before —
and After — You Remarry*

NEWLY UPDATED EDITION

Drs. Les & Leslie Parrott
#1 *New York Times* Bestselling Authors

ZONDERVAN

Saving Your Second Marriage Before It Starts Workbook for Men
Copyright © 2001, 2006, 2015 by Les and Leslie Parrott

This title is also available as a Zondervan ebook. Visit www.zondervan.com/ebooks.

Requests for information should be addressed to:
Zondervan, 3900 *Sparks Dr. SE, Grand Rapids, Michigan 49546*

ISBN 978-0-310-87559-8

Published in association with Yates & Yates, www.yates2.com.

Cover design: Ranjy Thomas / Flying Rhino
Cover photography: Surkov Vladimir / Shutterstock®
Interior design: Kait Lampher

First printing September 2015 / Printed in the United States of America

CONTENTS

SESSIONS

For Group or Couple Discussion with the Group Video Series

HOW TO USE THIS WORKBOOK

WE HAVE SEEN MANY COUPLES who marry and then wait to see what will happen. This workbook is a tool to help you make the *right* things happen. Its brief exercises and activities, to be completed as you read through *Saving Your Second Marriage Before It Starts*, come from our work in counseling couples and are proven strategies for enriching and developing your relationship. Too often, reading a book can lead to great ideas, but little action. This workbook will help you put feet on the ideas and put them into action. And we believe you will enjoy it! As Shakespeare said, "Joy's soul lies in the doing."

TAKE THE SYMBIS ASSESSMENT

If you haven't done so already, we want to encourage you to take the SYMBIS Assessment. It's a perfect accompaniment to your workbook exercises. It takes just thirty minutes to complete online (each of you answers questions separately) and provides a powerful and personalized fifteen-page report. You'll discover your unique strengths as a couple and how your two personalities mesh. In short, the SYMBIS Assessment gives you every possible advantage for launching lifelong love, and it's sure to take your relationship to a deeper level of intimacy.

In fact, if you purchased the book, *Saving Your Second Marriage Before It Starts*, you can use the unique code (specific to the book) to obtain a discount.

Because the SYMBIS Assessment is so robust, you'll need a certified SYMBIS Facilitator to guide you through your results.*

Using the assessment is not required. It's simply an option. But we believe it is truly one of the best ways to make the content of the book and the exercises in this workbook deeply relevant to your relationship. If you are interested, simply go to SYMBISassessment. com to learn more.

You will also find several places in this workbook where we will point you to a particular section of your SYMBIS Assessment Report if you happen to be using it.

WHY IT'S IDEAL FOR EACH OF YOU TO HAVE YOUR OWN WORKBOOK

This workbook is to be used in conjunction with your partner—whether you're dating, engaged or newly married. There is one workbook designed for men and one for women, and it is important that each of you have your own copy. For the best results, each of you should work on the exercises separately, then meet together to discuss your answers. We know from working with countless couples that many of these exercises can serve as a potential epiphany for you—a real eye-opener—if you answer honestly (not trying to guess what your partner *wants* you to say).

This is why you'll get the most from these experiences if you each have your own copy of the workbook. In many places your answers would be influenced by seeing what your partner wrote and thus diminish the value of the exercise. In addition, the men's and women's workbooks are contextualized to each gender, and this one even has specific content for you as a man.

---

* If you are already working with a counselor or pastor and they are not certified, we can help them become certified to use the assessment with you. They can do so at SYMBISassessment.com.

THE BEST APPROACH TO THESE EXERCISES

While there is no one right way to use this workbook, we suggest that you complete the exercises as you encounter them in the book, or soon after you have finished reading the chapter that covers the exercise. In other words, try to complete the exercises for that chapter before moving on to the next one. The point is to integrate the exercises into the process of reading the book. Some of the exercises are designed to be used again and again, helping you continue to improve your communication, for example, or deepen your sense of intimacy. Others are more of a one-shot exercise and are exploratory in nature.

In some cases, if you're using the SYMBIS Assessment, you may be using the workbooks with a SYMBIS Facilitator who will assign particular exercises as activities in between your sessions. And if you are debriefing your SYMBIS Assessment in a small group or class, you may use some of these exercises within the sessions themselves.

A NOTE ABOUT WORDING

We've designed these exercises to be appropriate for you—whether you are seriously dating, engaged, or already married. So don't get hung up on the use of "husband/wife" if you aren't married yet. We've done our best to avoid awkward phrasing while still acknowledging your relationship status. For example, we may say "partner" instead of "fiancé" or "spouse," etc.

USING THESE WORKBOOKS LONG-DISTANCE

If you and your partner are not in close proximity at this time, you can still do these exercises together. In fact, we have heard from countless couples who are in the military or located in different cities for various reasons during their engagement period or early years of marriage, and they love doing these exercises long-distance. They create a meaningful point of connection even when miles separate you.

As you navigate through the pages of this workbook, make it your own. Don't get too hung up on following the rules. If a particular exercise leads you down a more intriguing path, take it. Some of these exercises may simply serve as a springboard to discussions that fit your style more appropriately. However, if an exercise seems a bit challenging, don't give up on it. As the saying goes, anything worth having is worth working for. In any case, the goal of this workbook is not simply to fortify your reading of *Saving Your Second Marriage Before It Starts* — the goal is to apply it to your relationship, to make it stick.

A QUICK NOTE
TO LEADERS

We know that many leaders use these his/her workbooks to augment their sessions with couples. That's fantastic. With that in mind, we want to be sure you are aware of two resources that can be particularly helpful to you and the couples you serve.

If you are a certified SYMBIS Facilitator, you already know that the exercises in this workbook fit hand in glove with the personalized content found in the SYMBIS Assessment. If you are a minister, counselor or marriage mentor couple and you are not yet certified as a SYMBIS Facilitator, you can become one in no time. Simply visit SYMBISassessment.com for more information on how you can begin your training.

If you are leading a group or class of couples, the DVD kit that accompanies *Saving Your Second Marriage Before It Starts* can be especially helpful. For this reason, we have included a "Discussion Guide" in the later portion of these workbooks. The materials in your DVD kit as well as the resources in your online dashboard as a SYMBIS Facilitator will provide you with more guidance on optimizing your group experiences.

EXERCISES

28 Self-Tests to Put the Book into Action

THE REMARRIAGE MOTIVATION TEST

ON A SCALE OF 1 TO 10, rate how much of a factor each of the following motivators are for you to get married. Take time to consider each item, and be as honest as possible.

1. Love at first sight is a factor in why I'm ready to get married again.

Not at All True   Extremely True of Me

| 1 | 2 | 3 | 4 | 5 | 6 | 7 | 8 | 9 | 10 |

2. Rebounding from the pain of a previous marriage is a factor in my motivation for this second marriage.

Not at All True   Extremely True of Me

| 1 | 2 | 3 | 4 | 5 | 6 | 7 | 8 | 9 | 10 |

3. Rebellion against my ex-wife is a factor in my motivation.

Not at All True   Extremely True of Me

| 1 | 2 | 3 | 4 | 5 | 6 | 7 | 8 | 9 | 10 |

4. Loneliness contributes to my reasons for getting married again.

Not at All True   Extremely True of Me

| 1 | 2 | 3 | 4 | 5 | 6 | 7 | 8 | 9 | 10 |

5. A sense of obligation is a factor in motivating me to marry.

Not at All True   Extremely True of Me

| 1 | 2 | 3 | 4 | 5 | 6 | 7 | 8 | 9 | 10 |

6. Financial advancement is a part of my decision to get remarried.

Not at All True   Extremely True of Me

| 1 | 2 | 3 | 4 | 5 | 6 | 7 | 8 | 9 | 10 |

7. Sexual attraction is a factor driving me to get married at this time.

Not at All True   Extremely True of Me

| 1 | 2 | 3 | 4 | 5 | 6 | 7 | 8 | 9 | 10 |

8. Escape from an unhappy first marriage is causing me to want to get married again.

Not at All True   Extremely True of Me

| 1 | 2 | 3 | 4 | 5 | 6 | 7 | 8 | 9 | 10 |

9. Pressure from others has something to do with why I am getting married again.

Not at All True   Extremely True of Me

| 1 | 2 | 3 | 4 | 5 | 6 | 7 | 8 | 9 | 10 |

Scoring: Add up your score from each of the nine items. There are 90 possible points on this test. Add 10 to your score. If your score is 50 or less, you can rest easy in the fact that you are probably not getting remarried for some of the most common negative reasons. If your score is greater than 50, you will certainly want to do some soul-searching on your own and with your partner about the items that you ranked highest. We also strongly suggest talking about these motivators with an objective counselor.

THE REMARRIAGE READINESS QUESTIONNAIRE

IF YOU HAVE TAKEN the SYMBIS Assessment (SYMBISassessment.com), this particular exercise will look familiar. The SYMBIS Assessment Report presents the content of this exercise in a far more personalized format. If you're not using the SYMBIS Assessment, however, you will still benefit significantly from this workbook version of the exercise.

The following questions will help you assess your readiness for remarriage. Be ruthlessly honest with yourself while answering these questions.

1. Do you know who you are and do you like who you are?

2. Would you say you generally have a healthy sense of self-esteem and confidence?

3. Do you feel comfortable talking about your differences in times of conflict (rather than ignoring them)?

4. Are you twenty years of age or older?

5. Are you twenty-four years of age or older?

6. Would people you respect say you are personally mature?

7. Would you say you have resolved most of the ugly issues with your former wife?

8. Do you feel comfortable thinking for yourself and making your own decisions?

9. Are you able to make decisions without feeling compelled to please others?

10. Are you genuinely prepared to make your marriage relationship of utmost priority?

11. Have you resolved painful or other troubling issues with your past that are bound to impact your new marriage?

12. Have you identified specific quirks or qualities you may be bringing into your marriage as a result of your previous relationship?

13. Have you dated your partner for a year or more?

14. Have you dated your partner for two years or more?

15. Are you willing to take your time in determining whether your relationship is really ready for marriage?

16. Would you characterize your relationship as stable and steadfast?

17. Do you both practice compromise and negotiation effectively in your relationship?

18. Can you both resolve conflict between you without losing control?

19. Are you 100 percent committed, beyond a shadow of a doubt, to making this relationship work?

20. Do you fully agree with your partner's important goals and values?

21. Do you and your partner share many similarities (e.g., sense of humor, habits, goals)?

22. Are your differences tiny compared to your similarities?

23. Do you and your partner have similar family backgrounds?

24. Do you and your partner refrain from criticizing, correcting, or trying to "fix" each other?

25. Do you like this person as she is at this moment (as compared to expecting her to change)?

Scoring: Add up the number of yes responses from these items and multiply by four. That will give you a possible score of 100. If you answered honestly and your score is 90 or higher, your answers indicate you are probably ready for remarriage. A score of 80 to 89 indicates that you are on your way but would probably be wise to give it more time and careful counsel. A score of 79 or lower indicates that you still have a great deal of work to do before you are ready for remarriage. You are likely to benefit from the help of a good counselor and more time. Whether your score is high or low, this brief self-report assessment should serve simply as a guideline, not as the final answer.

YOUR PERSONAL TEN COMMANDMENTS

THIS EXERCISE IS DESIGNED to help you uncover some of your unspoken rules. It will take about fifteen to twenty minutes.

Try to articulate some of the unspoken rules you grew up with. Take your time to think it over. These unspoken rules are generally so ingrained that we are rarely aware of them. If you're not married yet, by the way, you may have discovered some of your "rules" with a previous roommate.

We've provided you with sections to stimulate your thinking. The best way to come up with your own commandments is to think of what "unspoken rules" you grew up with in your family.

RULES ABOUT FINANCES

Example: "Credit cards are to be used only in an emergency."

1. _____

_____

2. _____

_____

RULES ABOUT MEALTIME

Example: "Dinner should be served at the same time every night."

3.

4.

RULES ABOUT CHORES

Example: "The towels from the laundry should be folded in thirds (not in half)."

5.

6.

RULES ABOUT OTHER TRADITIONS AND HOLIDAYS

Example: "You should open presents on Christmas Eve (not Christmas morning)."

7.

8.

RULES ABOUT QUIRKY THINGS

Example: "Never put a bottle of ketchup on the table (put it in a dish)."

9. ....

....

10. ....

....

Once both of you have written your "personal ten commandments," share them with each other.

As a man, think about how your dad modeled certain behaviors in each of these areas and consider how this may shape your expectations as a husband.

What surprises you about your partner's rules and why? Do some of her rules cause you to immediately push back?

Are there any specific rules you would like to change (on your side or hers)?

The more you talk about your unspoken rules, the less likely they are to affect your marriage in a negative way.

In addition, here's a helpful tip. Any time you have a fight or disagreement, ask yourself, "Is this fight a result of one of us breaking an unspoken rule?" If so, add that rule to your list and discuss how you will handle that situation in the future.

Exercise Four

MAKING YOUR ROLES CONSCIOUS

If you are using the SYMBIS Assessment, a portion of a page of your fifteen-page report personalizes the results of this particular workbook exercise, so you may want to refer to that page now. Either way, this exercise will help you evaluate role expectations in your own terms and then compare your expectations with your partner's.

Following is a list of chores or life tasks that will need to be handled by you or your fiancée (wife). To make your unconscious understanding of roles conscious, first indicate how your parents handled these tasks. If they shared the task, then check both boxes. Then write down how you would like to divide the tasks, according to your understanding of your own and your partner's interests, time, and abilities. If you expect to share the task, check both boxes. Finally, compare your list with your partner's list and discuss the results. Put your joint decision of who will do what in the last column, and be prepared to renegotiate when your circumstances change. This exercise will take about twenty to thirty minutes.

	Your Mother	Your Father	You	Your Spouse	Final Decision
Providing income	☐	☐	☐	☐	_____
Staying home with children	☐	☐	☐	☐	_____
Paying bills and handling finances	☐	☐	☐	☐	_____
Yard work	☐	☐	☐	☐	_____
Gassing up the car	☐	☐	☐	☐	_____
Automobile maintenance	☐	☐	☐	☐	_____
Fixing things around the house	☐	☐	☐	☐	_____
Laundry	☐	☐	☐	☐	_____
Making the bed	☐	☐	☐	☐	_____
Doing the dishes	☐	☐	☐	☐	_____
Cleaning	☐	☐	☐	☐	_____
Cooking and baking	☐	☐	☐	☐	_____
Taking out the trash	☐	☐	☐	☐	_____
Grocery shopping	☐	☐	☐	☐	_____
Caring for a pet	☐	☐	☐	☐	_____
Scheduling social events	☐	☐	☐	☐	_____
Maintaining ties with friends and relatives	☐	☐	☐	☐	_____
Planning vacations	☐	☐	☐	☐	_____
Talking about spiritual matters	☐	☐	☐	☐	_____
Decorating the house	☐	☐	☐	☐	_____
Making major decisions	☐	☐	☐	☐	_____

	Your Mother	Your Father	You	Your Spouse	Final Decision
Initiating discussion about the relationship	☐	☐	☐	☐	_____
Keeping the house neat and orderly	☐	☐	☐	☐	_____
Disciplining the children	☐	☐	☐	☐	_____
Shopping for other needs	☐	☐	☐	☐	_____
Other _____	☐	☐	☐	☐	_____
Other _____	☐	☐	☐	☐	_____

Once you have both filled out this list, compare notes and answer these three questions together:

1. What role behaviors do you tend to agree upon?

2. What role behaviors do you tend to see quite differently?

3. How are you going to adjust your expectations on the role behaviors where you are currently not in sync?

Exercise Five

FROM IDEALIZING TO REALIZING YOUR PARTNER

THIS EXERCISE IS DESIGNED to help you relinquish unrealistic ideals you might hold about your partner and to discover her true character. It will take about twenty to thirty minutes.

Begin by rating on a 1 to 7 scale (1 being lowest and 7 being highest) how much the following traits describe you and your partner. Complete the first two columns ("Your Rating of You" and then "Your Rating of Your Wife"). Don't worry about the other two columns just yet.

Your Rating of You		Your Rating of Your Wife		Your Wife's Actual Rating		The Difference
___	Compassionate	___	-	___	=	___
___	Patient	___	-	___	=	___
___	Secure	___	-	___	=	___
___	Nurturing	___	-	___	=	___
___	Insightful	___	-	___	=	___
___	Confident	___	-	___	=	___
___	Relaxed	___	-	___	=	___
___	Tender	___	-	___	=	___
___	Even tempered	___	-	___	=	___

Your Rating of You		Your Rating of Your Wife	Your Wife's Actual Rating	The Difference
___	Honest	___ -	___ =	___
___	Healthy	___ -	___ =	___
___	Spiritual	___ -	___ =	___
___	Consistent	___ -	___ =	___

Once you have rated the first two columns, share your rating with each other and write them on your own page. Then subtract your partner's actual rating of herself from your rating of her. Note any significant differences and discuss them.

Our three biggest differences in this exercise are:

1. _____

_____

2. _____

_____

3. _____

_____

One of the central tasks of the early marriage years is to move from "idealizing" your wife to "realizing" your wife. How accurate is your image of who your wife is compared to who she really is? The more accurately you can present yourselves to each other, the easier your first years of marriage will be.

EXPLORING UNFINISHED BUSINESS

MARRIAGE IS NOT A QUICK FIX for avoiding your own personal problems. In fact, marriage may even intensify those problems. This exercise is designed to help you honestly face the psychological and spiritual work you need to do as a person so that you do not look to your wife to fulfill needs that she cannot. It will take about twenty to thirty minutes.

Everyone has yearnings that were seldom, if ever, fulfilled in their relationship with their parents. Take a moment to reflect, and then write down some of the needs and desires you felt that were never really fulfilled by your parents. We've provided you with a few headings to stimulate your thinking, but don't let that limit you to just these categories.

UNFULFILLED NEEDS FOR ENCOURAGEMENT

Example: "My parents never really encouraged my dreams or goals."

_____

_____

_____

UNFULFILLED NEEDS FOR PRAISE

Example: "My parents never really celebrated my successes."

UNFULFILLED NEEDS FOR LISTENING

Example: "My parents never really understood me for who I am."

UNFULFILLED NEEDS FOR FUN

Example: "My parents often thought I wasn't serious enough and wanted me to be more 'goal oriented.'"

OTHER UNFULFILLED NEEDS THAT SHAPE MY EXPECTATIONS

Example: "I've never had anyone in my life who appreciates my creativity."

_____

_____

_____

When we marry, we long to recreate the love and closeness and nurturance that we experienced or wished we had experienced in our relationship with our parents. But marriage is not always the place for those yearnings to be fulfilled. No human can meet another person's every need; deep relational longings are ultimately met only in a relationship with God.

If you are willing, share your writing with your partner and discuss the baggage you are both bringing into your marriage—and how your expectations of her as your wife might be shaped by your "unfinished business."

ASSESSING YOUR SELF-IMAGE

THIS EXERCISE IS DESIGNED to help you measure your self-image and construct an interdependent relationship with your wife. It will take about twenty to thirty minutes.

"You cannot love another person unless you love yourself." Most of us have heard that statement so often we tend to dismiss it as just another catchphrase in the lexicon of pop psychology. But a solid sense of self-esteem is a vital element in building the capacity to love.

The following self-test can give you a quick evaluation of your self-esteem. Answer each with "yes," "usually," "seldom," or "no."

1. Do you believe strongly in certain values and principles, enough that you are willing to defend them?

Yes	Usually	Seldom	No

2. Do you act on your own best judgment, without regretting your actions if others disapprove?

Yes	Usually	Seldom	No

3. Do you avoid worrying about what is coming tomorrow or fussing over yesterday's or today's mistakes?

Yes	Usually	Seldom	No

4. Do you have confidence in your general ability to deal with problems, even in the face of failures and setbacks?

Yes	Usually	Seldom	No

5. Do you feel generally equal — neither inferior nor superior — to others?

Yes	Usually	Seldom	No

6. Do you take it more or less for granted that other people are interested in you and value you?

Yes	Usually	Seldom	No

7. Do you accept praise without pretense or false modesty, and accept compliments without feeling guilty?

Yes	Usually	Seldom	No

8. Do you resist the efforts of others to dominate you, especially your peers?

Yes	Usually	Seldom	No

9. Do you accept the idea — and admit to others — that you are capable of feeling a wide range of impulses and desires, ranging from anger to love, sadness to happiness, resentment to acceptance? (It does not follow, however, that you will act on all these feelings and desires.)

Yes	Usually	Seldom	No

10. Do you genuinely enjoy yourself in a wide range of activities, including work, play, creative self-expression, companionship, and just plain loafing?

Yes	Usually	Seldom	No

11. Do you sense and consider the needs of others?

Yes	Usually	Seldom	No

If your answer to most of the questions is "yes" or "usually," it's an indication that you have a sturdy sense of self-esteem. If most of your answers are "no" or "seldom," you may likely suffer from a low self-image and will need to strengthen it to build the best marriage. Research indicates that self-esteem has a lot to do with the way you will respond to your wife. People with a healthy self-image are more apt to express their opinions, are less sensitive to criticism, and are generally less preoccupied with themselves.

The point of this little self-test is not to accurately pinpoint your self-esteem. It's to generate a helpful discussion between the two of you. So, if you are willing, discuss your answers with each other and talk about how in reality you cannot make each other whole (though you can certainly help each other on the pathway to wholeness).

Exercise Eight

DEFINING LOVE

If you are using the SYMBIS Assessment, a portion of a page of your fifteen-page SYMBIS Report personalizes the results of this particular workbook exercise, so you may want to refer to that page now. Either way, this exercise will help you define love in your own terms and compare your definition with your partner's. It will take ten to fifteen minutes.

Researcher Beverly Fehr asked more than 170 people to rate the central features of love.

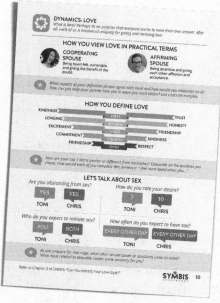

The twelve most important attributes they identified are listed below. Take a moment to prioritize this list for yourself by checkmarking the three qualities that are most important to you.

___ Acceptance	___ Interest in the other
___ Caring	___ Loyalty
___ Commitment	___ Respect
___ Concern for the other's well-being	___ Supportiveness
___ Friendship	___ Trust
___ Honesty	___ Wanting to be with the other

Next, write a brief definition of love that incorporates these qualities.

Love is . . .

_____

_____

_____

Now, compare your priorities and your definition with your partner's to see what differences, if any, you might have when it comes to defining love.

Finally, complete these sentences to get a better feel for the application of your definition of love:

I feel most loved when you . . .

_____

_____

_____

Though you may or may not know it, I'm showing you my love when I . . .

_____

_____

_____

If pertinent to you: My definition of love has changed in the following ways since my first marriage . . .

_____

_____

_____

Exercise Nine

GETTING YOUR SEX LIFE OFF TO A GREAT START

THIS EXERCISE IS DESIGNED to help you dispel some common myths about sex and become more knowledgeable about lovemaking as a married couple.*

Below is a true and false questionnaire for you to complete. Don't worry about getting the right answers. Simply answer each item the best you can.

T   F   The key to sexual fulfillment is simply to do what comes naturally. In other words, let your instincts be your guide.

T   F   Most normal married couples have sexual intercourse about two to three times a week.

T   F   Because men typically have a stronger sex drive than women, it is primarily the husband's job to initiate sex — not the wife's.

T   F   When it comes down to it, men are almost always ready and willing to have sex, and a good wife should always be available for it.

T   F   The best way for a woman to have an orgasm is during intercourse.

---

* We are indebted to Cliff and Joyce Penner and Louis and Melissa McBurney for the wealth of knowledge they provide in this area.

T   F   While men have just one orgasm during sex, a woman must have multiple orgasms to be fulfilled sexually.

T   F   A man's erection is a signal that he is going to need intercourse or ejaculation.

T   F   The normal position for sexual intercourse is with the man on top.

T   F   To reach ultimate sexual fulfillment, a couple should strive for simultaneous orgasms, where both the husband and wife climax at the same time.

T   F   In general, the larger the man's penis, the more pleasurable sex is for the woman.

Number of True answers: ____   Number of False answers: ____

Once you have totaled your answers, compare notes and go through the following correct answers together. What matters here is not whether you answered correctly—the point is to learn more accurate information about your sex life as a married couple.

T   F   The key to sexual fulfillment is simply to do what comes naturally. In other words, let your instincts be your guide.

While many believe that if you are really good at sex you don't have to learn about it, the truth is that good sex requires much more than just doing what comes naturally. Therefore, one of the best ways to improve your sex life after marriage and to really enjoy it is to educate yourselves, experiment with each other, and teach each other. For example, this may mean reading a book from time to time about sexual intimacy in marriage. The more you learn about sex as a couple, especially each other's preferences and desires, the better your sex life will be. So the answer to this item is false.

| T | F | Most normal married couples have sexual intercourse about two to three times a week. |

When it comes to the frequency of sexual intercourse in your marriage, the two of you determine what is normal. You may have sex twice a day or twice per month. What matters is that, over the course of your married life, you talk about the best balance of your two sexual desires. So the answer to this item is false.

| T | F | Because men typically have a stronger sex drive than women, it is primarily the husband's job to initiate sex — not the wife's. |

Women have sexual urges and thoughts just as men do. In fact, women tend to fantasize even more than men. When women learn to express their sexual urges directly and share their creative fantasies, their husbands are delighted and their sex life is sparked. So it's not up to the man to always initiate sex, and the answer to this item is false. By the way, since women can be more particular about where, when, and how they want to be touched, it takes pressure off the husband and produces greater pleasure for the wife if she also takes the lead.

| T | F | When it comes down to it, men are almost always ready and willing to have sex, and a good wife should always be available for it. |

Yikes! This false belief has led too many couples into trouble because it produces such incredible demand—on both partners. First, it demands that the husband behave as though he is interested even when he is not. And it also demands that the wife be responsive to her husband's arousal even when she is not interested. Truth be told, either one of you can decide to participate in a sexual time together when one of you is feeling the desire and the other is not, but it should not be by demand. Sex should always be a choice. As the Penners say, "Demand is a killer to a healthy, long-term sexual relationship."

T   F   The best way for a woman to have an orgasm is during intercourse.

Here's the truth: The majority of women do not have orgasms during intercourse. While any woman can learn to be orgasmic during intercourse if she desires to, most women respond orgasmically to manual clitoral stimulation. Of course, some women only respond during intercourse and others respond either way. All variations are delightful ways of receiving sexual pleasure and release, but have nothing to do with "the right way." What is right is what works for you. And keep in mind that the stimulation that triggers the orgasm in the woman has nothing to do with the man or his masculinity. As you both listen to your inner desires and communicate those desires to each other and respond to each other's invitations, the automatic response orgasm is more likely to happen. So the answer to this item is false.

T   F   While men have just one orgasm during sex, a woman must have multiple orgasms to be fulfilled sexually.

The number of orgasms a woman experiences during sex is not an indicator of her level of sexual fulfillment. Many women are totally satisfied after one release. Others quickly get restimulated and desire more. So, for the man, there's no need to equate the number of orgasms with his level of "performance." So the answer to this item is false.

T F   A man's erection is a signal that he is going to need intercourse or ejaculation.

An erection simply means a man is aroused and that's all. An erection for the man is no different than vaginal lubrication for the woman. It's not a demand for action, even though many men say they just cannot handle getting aroused and not having an ejaculation. The truth is that all men get erections every eighty to ninety minutes while they sleep, but these erections rarely lead to an ejaculation. It is equally possible to allow arousal to come and go during caressing or in response to seeing his wife's body. So, again, the answer to this item is false.

T F   The normal position for sexual intercourse is with the man
on top.

The man-on-top position is commonly used by many couples, but that does not make it the normal or right position. With more sexual experiences together in your marriage, you will discover positions that bring you the most pleasure. You need to feel free to try a variety of positions in your lovemaking. So the answer is false.

T F   To reach ultimate sexual fulfillment, a couple should strive
for simultaneous orgasms, where both the husband and
wife climax at the same time.

Having simultaneous orgasms can be fun if it happens, but it's an unnecessary goal to put on your lovemaking. It has absolutely nothing to do with how successful you are as a couple. The demand for both spouses to have orgasms at the same time gets in the way of the pleasure of enjoying each other. Many couples prefer separate orgasms so each one can experience the other's. So, again, the answer is false.

| T | F | In general, the larger the man's penis, the more pleasurable sex is for the woman. |

Penis size is the source of many myths. But in truth, it has nothing to do with a man's sexuality, his attractiveness to his wife, his skill as a lover, or the satisfaction he can bring to his wife. The quality of sex is not in any way related to penis size. When erect, penises vary little in size from one to another. A smaller, flaccid penis enlarges proportionately more when erect than does a larger flaccid penis. Also, the vagina adapts to the penis, and it is only in the outer third of the vagina that the woman responds to the penis. The shortest penis is more than adequate to bring pleasure to a woman. So the answer is false. The penis myths perpetuated by locker-room jokes have nothing to do with reality.

So, each of the ten items in this self-test is false. If you answered any of them as true, don't feel badly. Each of these items represents one of the most common myths about marital sex. And now that you know the truth, you are far more likely to get your sex life off to a great start.

Of course, to augment your sexual knowledge, you will also need a solid understanding of the male and female anatomy. You have probably already studied this in school, but even so, it's very helpful to brush up on this information. Cliff and Joyce Penner's bestselling book *The Gift of Sex* is a terrific resource for this, as is Louis and Melissa McBurney's book *Real Questions, Real Answers about Sex*.

We want to leave you with one more thought. Remember that one of the keys to a great sex life is to talk openly about it as husband and wife. Far too many married couples simply don't discuss their sex life together. Once you are married, we recommend that you talk in specific terms by completing such sentences as:

I feel sexually aroused by you when ...
When we are making love, I really enjoy ...
When we are making love, I feel uncomfortable when you ...

The surest turnoff for me is ...
The surest turn-on for me is ...
What you need to know about me when it comes to sex is ...

These kinds of specific statements will do wonders for your sex life right from the start and ensure "hot monogamy" for decades.

YOUR CHANGING LOVE STYLE

THIS EXERCISE WILL HELP YOU understand how love is not stagnant and how the love you have for each other will change during different life passages. It will take twenty-five to thirty minutes.

Using the triangular model of love described in chapter 3 of *Saving Your Second Marriage Before It Starts* (passion, intimacy, and commitment), draw how your love style with your partner has changed over time. You may want to divide your relationship into three phases and then draw the love triangle that best suits each phase. In other words, if early on passion was stronger than commitment and intimacy, draw a triangle (identifying each side) representing that, and so on.

First third of our relationship

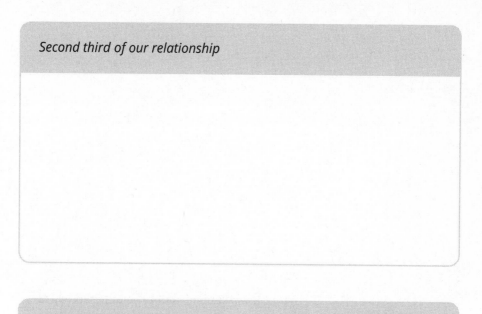

Second third of our relationship

Third third of our relationship

As we grow and develop, each stage of the life cycle is marked by the emergence of a new form of love. This means that during certain phases of life, some sides of the triangle will get more attention than others. Using the triangular model of love, on the next page draw how your love might look in future passages of marriage (e.g., how will it look in five years or even fifty years).

Discuss with your partner how you feel about the inevitability of love taking on different forms in your future.

CULTIVATING INTIMACY

THIS EXERCISE WILL HELP YOU open your heart and increase your level of intimacy.

Begin by writing about your shared experiences. What is it about your backgrounds that draws you together? What things set the two of you apart from others? What experiences have you had together that bring back fond memories?

Next, focus on things that the two of you share. Begin by jotting down one or two things in each of the following categories, then discuss them with your partner. The more detailed you can be, the better.

- Interests we have in common include:

  _____

  _____

  _____

- Plans we share for our future include:

  _____

  _____

  _____

- Fears and anxieties we both have include:

_____

_____

_____

- Hopes and dreams we share include:

_____

_____

_____

- Spiritual beliefs we both have include:

_____

_____

_____

Conclude this exercise by talking in specific terms about what the two of you can do to cultivate more emotional intimacy in your relationship.

LISTENING TO YOUR SELF-TALK

THIS EXERCISE WILL HELP YOU and your partner examine how much your attitude shapes the moods of your marriage. It will take about ten to fifteen minutes.

List three circumstances that typically get you into a rotten mood. For example: being stuck in traffic, waiting for someone who is late to arrive, having your credit card rejected, and so on.

1. _____

_____

2. _____

_____

3. _____

_____

There is a maxim in psychology that says "you feel what you think." In other words, your feelings are the result of what is going on in your mind. For each of the bad circumstances you listed above, write down what you are saying to yourself that makes you feel so rotten. For example: "I could be playing tennis instead of being stuck on this freeway."

1. _____

_____

2. _____

_____

3. _____

_____

Now, exercise your power to choose your own attitude by changing your self-talk. Write three alternative statements that would not lead to feeling so rotten. For example: "At least I can use this time to just relax and mentally rehearse my tennis serve."

1. _____

_____

2. _____

_____

3. _____

_____

Negative self-talk can also affect our responses to more serious situations. To see how negative self-talk may have affected you, list two situations in your life that were difficult or painful to deal with. For example: losing a job, breaking off a relationship, or going through a serious illness.

1. _____

_____

2. _____

_____

For each of the crises you listed above, write down things you said to yourself that added to your pain. For example: "I was fired from my job because I'm a natural-born loser."

1. _____

_____

2. _____

_____

Again, exercise your power to choose your own attitude by changing your self-talk. Write two alternative statements that did help or could have helped you adapt to the situation and grow through it. For example: "I will learn from my mistakes and, with God's help, make sure they don't happen again."

1. _____

_____

2. _____

_____

Talk about this exercise with your partner. Discuss how changing your self-talk can improve your chances for marital happiness. How can the two of you team up to fight negative self-talk?

Exercise Thirteen

AVOIDING THE BLAME GAME

THIS EXERCISE WILL HELP YOU and your partner take responsibility for your own attitudes. It will take about ten to fifteen minutes.

Below are several scenarios where blame typically enters the picture. For each scenario, decide on your own who is to blame.

FIRST SCENE

It's Valentine's Day. Mary has prepared a special meal for Dan— all his favorite foods. She also made him a special valentine. Dan, however, didn't get Mary anything. After dinner, Dan thanks Mary for the food and slumps into a chair in front of the television. Mary, feeling hurt, leaves the dirty dishes in the sink and goes into the bedroom to cry. Dan realizes what just happened, follows her into the bedroom, and the two accuse each other of being insensitive. Who is at fault?

Dan is to blame   Mary is to blame

SECOND SCENE

Aaron and Kim are having dinner with another couple. During the casual conversation, Kim jokingly makes fun of Aaron's shirt. He laughs at first but soon he becomes withdrawn, and the conversation becomes noticeably strained. When they get home, both of them accuse the other of ruining the evening. Who is at fault?

Aaron is to blame   Kim is to blame

THIRD SCENE

On a whim, Carl buys a new hi-def TV on sale. He and Michelle had talked about getting one, but they'd decided to wait another year. Carl, however, felt the bargain was too good to pass up and also thought it would be a nice surprise for Michelle. It wasn't. All Michelle could think about was how they were saving money for plane tickets to see her family at Christmas. Carl and Michelle blamed each other for being too controlling with their money. Who is at fault?

Carl is to blame   Michelle is to blame

You may now compare your answers with each other, but there are no "correct" responses. It doesn't matter who is to blame. It doesn't matter who is at fault. What matters in building a happy marriage is defining what the problem is and seeing how each of you can be a part of the solution. Take time to read through the scenarios again, placing yourselves in each couple's shoes. What could each of you do to avoid playing the blame game in these instances?

_____

_____

_____

_____

_____

_____

_____

ADJUSTING TO THINGS BEYOND YOUR CONTROL

IF YOU ARE USING the SYMBIS Assessment you may want to refer to the Dynamics: Attitude page of your personalized report as it relates to this particular workbook exercise. This one will help you and your partner more effectively adjust to the jolts of life. It will take about ten to fifteen minutes.

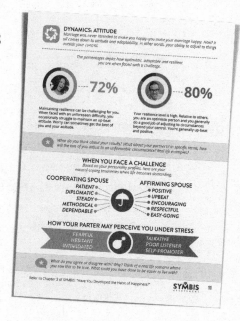

The book talked about how different the Christmas story would be if Mary and Joseph had not had the capacity to adjust to circumstances beyond their control. What situations or circumstances in your relationship (including your wedding if you are already married) have already thrown you for a loop? Jot down two or three particular challenges you did not anticipate:

_____

_____

_____

How did you respond to these unexpected situations? List some things you did to keep your chin up and some things you did that didn't work as well.

Positive Ways I Coped	Negative Ways I Coped

Now compare your coping strategies with your partner's. In what ways can the two of you improve your capacities to adjust? How can you be better equipped to maintain a positive outlook when similar unexpected circumstances arise in the future?

Conclude this exercise by discussing what will happen in your marriage if you do not practice your ability to adjust to things beyond your control.

Exercise Fifteen

HOW WELL DO YOU COMMUNICATE?

IF YOU ARE USING the SYMBIS Assessment you may want to refer to the Dynamics: Communication page of your report as it relates to your personal "talk styles." It will provide fuller context to this exercise which is designed to help you improve how well you communicate with your partner. It will take about ten minutes. Answer the questions as honestly as you can. The more honest you are, the more meaningful the exercise will be.

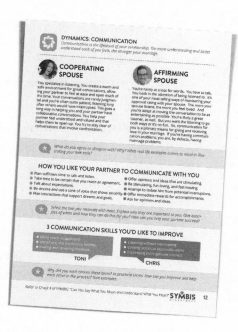

1. When your partner is in a bad mood, you are likely to:

   A. Ask whether she's getting her period.

   B. Leave her alone until she's feeling better.

   C. Ask her what's wrong.

2. She says you don't tell her often enough that you love her. You reply:

    A. "I tell you I love you all the time."

    B. "You know I love you. Why do I have to say it?"

    C. "I love you very much. Sometimes I just forget to say so."

3. You are watching television, and she says she'd like to talk to you. You say:

    A. "How about ten o'clock?"

    B. "Anytime you want."

    C. "Sorry, I'm in the middle of something right now."

4. How often do you win arguments with your partner?

    A. Almost always

    B. Almost never

    C. I try not to think in terms of winning or losing.

5. Your partner wants to talk about some difficulties she is having at work. Would you most likely:

    A. Point out that you have work problems of your own?

    B. Offer helpful advice?

    C. Listen and try to be supportive?

6. For the second time this week you find that she didn't run an errand as she had promised. Annoyed, you:

    A. Tell her how much it irritates you and do it yourself.

    B. Pout a bit and ask her to do it tomorrow.

    C. "Forget" to do something for her next time she asks.

7. You're in a romantic mood, but when you reach for her she just yawns. You:

A. Feel rejected and say, "Whew, it's cold in here."

B. Ask her why she isn't responding.

C. Let her know your desires but adjust if she is not in sync.

Scoring: For questions one, two, four, five, and seven, give yourself one point for each "A" answer, two for each "B," and three for each "C." Then on questions three and six, give yourself three points for each "A," two for each "B," and one for each "C."

7 to 11 points: Hiding your feelings is one of the fastest ways you can ruin a relationship. You need to learn how to listen to your partner and how to talk with her. Chapter 6 will show you how.

12 to 17 points: You're doing well, but you need to remember that your partner needs your support and encouragement much more than she needs your advice. You can really benefit from practicing some of the skills discussed in chapter 7.

18 to 21 points: You're doing quite well in the area of communication, but there's always room for improvement. Chapter 7 will help you fine-tune some skills you are already good at.

THE DAILY TEMPERATURE READING

THIS EXERCISE WILL HELP YOU and your partner maintain an easy flow of communication about the big and little things going on in your lives. It will take about thirty minutes.

At first this exercise may seem artificial and even hokey. But in time you'll evolve your own style and find that it is invaluable for staying close. Do it daily, perhaps during a meal. Here are the basics. Sit close, holding each other's hands (touch creates an atmosphere of acceptance), then follow these five steps:

1. *Appreciation.* Take turns expressing appreciation for something your partner has done. Thank each other.

_____

_____

2. *New Information.* In the absence of information, assumptions (often false ones) rush in. Tell your partner something new ("We finally got a new account executive at work"). Let your partner in on your life, and then listen to the news your partner shares.

_____

_____

3. *Puzzles.* Take turns asking each other something you don't understand but your partner can explain: "Why were you so down last night?" Or voice a concern about yourself: "I don't know why I got so angry while I was balancing the checkbook yesterday."

_____

_____

4. *Complaint with Request.* Without being judgmental, cite a specific behavior that bothers you and state the behavior you are asking for instead. "When you clean the top of the stove, please dry it with a paper towel. If you don't, it leaves streaks."

_____

_____

5. *Hopes.* Share your hopes, from the mundane ("I hope we have sunshine this weekend") to the grandiose ("I'd really love to spend a month in Europe with you").

_____

_____

These simple steps have worked for many couples who want to keep the channels of communication open.

I CAN HEAR CLEARLY NOW

YOUR PARTNER WILL OFTEN hide important feelings behind her words. Reflecting her feelings is one of the most helpful and difficult listening techniques to implement. Following are some statements that a wife might make. Read each separately, listening for feelings. Make note of the feeling you hear, and write out a response which reflects that feeling for each of the statements.

1. "I don't want your advice!"

_____

_____

2. "Karen doesn't seem to call me like she used to."

_____

_____

3. "I am so tired of never knowing when you are going to get home."

_____

_____

4. "I'd like to ask for a raise, but what if I don't get it?"

_____

_____

5. "Just once I'd like not to have to pick your coat off this chair."

_____

_____

Now compare your list of reflective statements to those listed below to see how accurately you recognized feelings. Give yourself a 2 on those items where your choice closely matches, a 1 on items where your choice only partially matches, and a 0 if you missed altogether.

Possible Responses to the Exercise in Active Listening:

1. "Sounds like you'd just like to be understood."
2. "You must feel kind of hurt."
3. "You sound so frustrated; let's work this thing out."
4. "Sounds like you are feeling anxious and a little afraid."
5. "That's got to be aggravating. I'll make it a point not to do that so much."

How You Rate on Recognizing Feelings:

8–10   Above average recognition of feelings
5–7   Average recognition of feelings
0–4   Below average recognition of feelings

Exercise Eighteen

COUPLE'S INVENTORY

THIS EXERCISE WILL HELP YOU take stock of the roles you both play, consciously and unconsciously, in your relationship. It will take about twenty to thirty minutes.

Complete the following sentences as honestly as you can.

1. I am important to our marriage because _____

_____

_____

2. What I contribute to my partner's success is _____

_____

_____

3. I feel central to our relationship when _____

_____

_____

4. I feel peripheral to our relationship when _____

_____

_____

5. The ways I have fun with you are _____

_____

_____

6. The way I get space for myself in our relationship is _____

_____

_____

7. The ways I am intimate with you are _____

_____

_____

8. The role I play as your husband is _____

_____

_____

9. I feel most masculine in our relationship when _____

_____

_____

10. I deal with stress by _____

_____

_____

11. The division of labor in household tasks is decided by _____

_____

_____

12. Our finances are controlled by _____

_____

_____

13. How we spend our spare time is determined by _____

_____

_____

14. Our social life is planned by _____

_____

_____

15. I need you to _____

_____

_____

Compare your statements with each other and discuss how being a man influences the way you responded.

YOUR TOP TEN NEEDS

IF YOU ARE USING the SYMBIS
Assessment you may want to refer
to the Dynamics: Gender page of
your personalize report as it relates
to this exercise. Either way, this
workbook exercise will help you
identify some of your deepest
needs in a marriage relationship
and communicate those needs to
your partner. It will take about
twenty to thirty minutes.

Listed below are some of the
most common needs that people
identify as being important in
marriage. Rate how important each of these items is for you. If you
wish to add other items not included in our list, please do so. As
always, do this on your own before discussing it with your partner.

	Not that important						Very important
Admiration	1	2	3	4	5	6	7
Affection	1	2	3	4	5	6	7
Commitment	1	2	3	4	5	6	7
Companionship	1	2	3	4	5	6	7
Conversation	1	2	3	4	5	6	7
Financial support	1	2	3	4	5	6	7
Honesty	1	2	3	4	5	6	7
Intimacy	1	2	3	4	5	6	7
Personal space	1	2	3	4	5	6	7
Respect	1	2	3	4	5	6	7
Rootedness	1	2	3	4	5	6	7
Security	1	2	3	4	5	6	7
Sex	1	2	3	4	5	6	7
Shared activities	1	2	3	4	5	6	7
_____	1	2	3	4	5	6	7
_____	1	2	3	4	5	6	7

Now that you have completed rating the needs, rank them in order of importance. Next, share the results with your partner.

What needs do both of you identify as important?

Discuss what needs are most important to you personally. As you discuss them, explain what that need means to you. Men and women often mean different things even when they use the same word (e.g., intimacy).

Finally, discuss how each of your needs might change as you grow in marriage.

IDENTIFYING YOUR HOT TOPICS

THIS EXERCISE WILL HELP YOU PUT your finger on those issues that are especially prone to cause conflict in your relationship. It will take about twenty minutes. And if you are using the SYMBIS Assessment, you'll see this spelled out in personalized terms on the Dynamics: Conflict page of your report.

Listed below are the common relationship issues that most couples will encounter from time to time over the course of the relationship. Rate how much of a problem each issue is for you right now. If you wish to add other areas not included in our list, please do so. As always, do this on your own before discussing it with your partner.

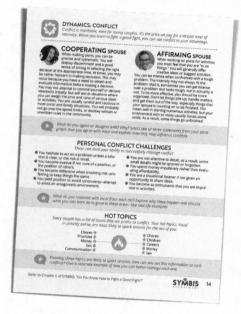

	Not at all a problem					Very much a problem	
Careers	1	2	3	4	5	6	7
Children	1	2	3	4	5	6	7
Chores	1	2	3	4	5	6	7
Communication	1	2	3	4	5	6	7
Friends	1	2	3	4	5	6	7
Illness	1	2	3	4	5	6	7
In-laws	1	2	3	4	5	6	7
Jealousy	1	2	3	4	5	6	7
Money	1	2	3	4	5	6	7
Priorities	1	2	3	4	5	6	7
Recreation	1	2	3	4	5	6	7
Relatives	1	2	3	4	5	6	7
Religion	1	2	3	4	5	6	7
Sex	1	2	3	4	5	6	7
Sleep habits	1	2	3	4	5	6	7
_____	1	2	3	4	5	6	7
_____	1	2	3	4	5	6	7

Now that you have completed rating the issues, share the results with your partner. What issues are "hot" for both of you, and what issues are "hot" for one or the other of you? Next, discuss which issues might become more troublesome in the future and what you can do to calm the conflict before it erupts.

MONEY TALKS AND SO CAN WE

THIS EXERCISE WILL HELP YOU delve into money matters that will impact your marriage in countless ways. It may take a bit longer than some of the other exercises in this workbook, but it is immensely practical and will benefit you for decades.

YOUR FAMILY AND MONEY

You already know from earlier exercises that your family of origin shapes nearly everything you do. And how you relate to money is not an exception. So let's begin by having you simply note how money was treated, valued, and managed in your home growing up. How did your childhood shape your beliefs about money? Make a few notes here so that you can discuss it in a moment with your partner. Be sure to note how you think you are similar or different than your parents when it comes to money matters. And also note how you see money being managed in your home together.

THE MONEY SELF-TEST

What follows is a series of statements for you to rate. There are no right or wrong answers, and don't try to answer how you think others might want you to. Be honest. This is a self-test that will help you and your partner get real about personal finances.

1. I feel comfortable talking about finances with my partner.

Never	Rarely	Sometimes	Often	Always

2. I pay bills on time.

Never	Rarely	Sometimes	Often	Always

3. I pay off my credit card balance every month.

Never	Rarely	Sometimes	Often	Always

4. I save a portion of my income every month.

Never	Rarely	Sometimes	Often	Always

5. I give a predetermined portion of my money to charities or my church every month.

Never	Rarely	Sometimes	Often	Always

6. I manage my money with a set budget that I follow.

Never	Rarely	Sometimes	Often	Always

7. I buy things on impulse.

Never	Rarely	Sometimes	Often	Always

8. Most people who know me well would say I'm a saver and rather tight with my money.

Never	Rarely	Sometimes	Often	Always

9. I know how much I have in my bank account at almost any given time.

Never	Rarely	Sometimes	Often	Always

10. I regularly keep track of what I spend and where I spend it.

Never	Rarely	Sometimes	Often	Always

11. When it comes to investing, I give serious thought to and study how I can invest my money for high returns in the long run.

Never	Rarely	Sometimes	Often	Always

Once you have completed this self-test, take a few minutes to talk with your partner about money matters. Begin by discussing how your families approached finances. And keep in mind that this discussion is simply about getting money matters on the table. It's not about judging each other's approaches. And as you compare your answers on your two self-tests, note each item where your answers are quite divergent.

Here are a few questions to help you organize your findings:

1. Do you have the same or different views on spending styles, credit, and debt?

_____

_____

2. Your views on giving and saving money and investing for the future?

_____

_____

3. Your views on working with a financial plan and budget?

_____

_____

DO YOU CLASH OVER CASH?

After this discussion, rank on the following continuum where the two of you might fall when it comes to money matters:

Out of sync   In sync

| 1 | 2 | 3 | 4 | 5 | 6 | 7 | 8 | 9 | 10 |

Don't be disturbed if you find you have many divergent views on finances as a couple. Most couples do. What matters is what you are going to do about it. What follows are practical suggestions to help you begin implementing a proven plan.

IF EITHER ONE OF YOU IS IN DEBT, START DIGGING OUT

If you haven't done so already, each of you needs to be up front with the other about where you are personally on your finances as it relates to debt. We've seen many couples who get married only to discover that their partner has a significant amount of debt that was never disclosed beforehand. Don't allow this to happen to you, and don't hold back this kind of information from your partner. You will wrestle with trust issues for decades as a result of not being up front early on. And it's simple. It basically involves answering three primary questions:

1. Do you have credit card debt? If so, how much?
2. Do you have loans you are paying off? If so, how much?
3. Do you owe anyone money? If so, how much?

Now if either of you has financial debt, you need to devise a plan together for getting out of it as soon as possible. If the debt is significant, this may mean talking with a financial consultant who specializes in these matters. One of the most respected and successful do-it-yourself programs comes from Dave Ramsey, and you can visit his website at www.daveramsey.com. You'll want to implement a cash control system, for example, and you will find all the tools you need for this at his site. Digging out of debt is the first order of business in getting on your feet financially as a couple.

DESIGN A BUDGET

Whether you have debt or not, we strongly recommend that you design a budget together as a couple. Why? Because a budget allows you to control your money rather than the other way around. And it's not as bad as you might imagine. It begins by getting an accurate picture of your total income and then deciding how you will allocate it. Of course, this may be revised as circumstances change, but you've got to start somewhere. If you're working with a SYMBIS Facilitator, they can provide you with an Excel version of the budget worksheet that does all the math for you. If not, here's a budget worksheet that will help you get going:

Basic Budget Worksheet

CATEGORY	MONTHLY BUDGET AMOUNT	MONTHLY ACTUAL AMOUNT	DIFFERENCE BETWEEN ACTUAL AND BUDGET
INCOME:			
Salary/Wages			
Bonuses			
Investment Income			
Miscellaneous Income			
INCOME SUBTOTAL			
EXPENSES:			
Mortgage or Rent			
TV Cable			
Telephone			
Home Repairs/ Maintenance			
Car Payments			
Gasoline/Oil			
Auto Repairs/ Maintenance/Fees			
Other Transportation (tolls, bus, subway, etc.)			
Child Care			
Auto Insurance			

CATEGORY	MONTHLY BUDGET AMOUNT	MONTHLY ACTUAL AMOUNT	DIFFERENCE BETWEEN ACTUAL AND BUDGET
Home Owner's/ Renter's Insurance			
Computer Expense			
Entertainment/ Recreation			
Groceries			
Toiletries/Household Products			
Clothing			
Eating Out			
Tithe/Donations			
Health Care (medical/ dental/ vision, incl. insurance)			
Hobbies			
Interest Expense (mortgage, credit cards, fees)			
Magazines/ Newspapers			
Federal Income Tax			
State Income Tax			
Social Security/ Medicare Tax			
Personal Property Tax			
Pets			
Miscellaneous Expenses			
EXPENSES SUBTOTAL			

NET INCOME (INCOME LESS EXPENSES)			

Here's How to Use This Worksheet:

- Go through your checkbook or bills for the last two to three months and add and delete categories from the worksheet to fit your expenditures.

- Think about your hobbies and your habits and be sure to add categories for these expenses.

- Go through your pay stubs and calculate your average monthly gross pay. Do the same for any interest income, dividends, bonuses, or other miscellaneous income.

- For each expense category, try to determine a budget amount that realistically reflects your actual expenses while setting targeted spending levels that will enable you to save money.

- If an expense is incurred more or less often than monthly, convert it to a monthly amount when calculating the monthly budget amount. For instance, an auto expense that is billed every six months would be converted to monthly by dividing the six-month premium by six.

- Once you're comfortable with your expense categories and budgeted amounts, enter expenditures from your checkbook from the last month.

- Keep track of cash expenditures throughout the month and total and categorize these at the end of each month.

- Subtotal the income and expense categories. Subtract the total expenses from the total income to arrive at your net income.

- If the number is negative, your expenses are greater than your income. Your situation can probably be greatly improved by changing your spending habits.

- After you've tracked your actual spending for a month or two, analyze your spending to identify where you can comfortably make cuts.

- Once you've gotten the budgeting process in place, take an in-depth look at your largest spending categories, brainstorm about ways to reduce spending in specific categories, and set realistic goals.

Keep this in mind: One of the top reasons, if not *the* top reason, so many people fail at budgeting is attitude. If you think of it as a penny-pinching sacrifice instead of a means for achieving your financial goals and dreams, how long are you likely to stick with it? Many people refuse to budget because of budgeting's negative connotation. If you're one of these people, try thinking of it as a "spending plan" instead of a "budget." It's like the difference between going on a diet and eating healthily. One is negative and restrictive; the other is positive and allows you to indulge now and then and still achieve your goals.

TALK ABOUT YOUR FINANCIAL GOALS

Throughout your marriage you will talk about financial goals from time to time, but this is an important topic at the start as well. So take another moment or two to consider where you and your partner would like to be financially in another year, another five years, ten years, and so on. Here are some questions to generate this discussion:

1. What are your thoughts on owning your own home?
2. Have you considered how your finances will be impacted by having children?
3. Do you have a plan for paying off car loans?
4. What are your goals when it comes to giving money away and supporting causes you believe in?

If you are using the SYMBIS Assessment you will want to also refer to the Money Matrix personalized report. It provides an even deeper experience of some of the financial issues explored in this workbook exercise.

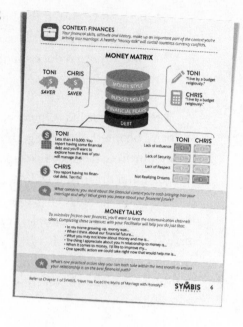

Exercise Twenty-Two

MIND READING

THIS EXERCISE WILL HELP YOU bring true and false assumptions you are making about your partner into the open so there are fewer surprises and conflicts. It will take about ten minutes.

Normally, trying to "mind read" what your partner is thinking is not a healthy habit (because it will lead you to jump to irrational conclusions). That's why in this exercise you will actually assess the accuracy of your assumptions before acting on them.

Here's how it works. The next time you sense that your partner is upset with you, pause for a moment and say, "I want to read your mind." Then tell her what you think she was saying to herself. For example, "I think you are mad about the way I left the bed this morning," or "I think you are upset because I wanted to watch TV instead of take a walk." Then say, "How accurate am I?" Your partner can then rate how accurate you are on a percentage scale. For example, she might say, "That's about 20 percent accurate," or "That's 100 percent accurate."

This simple exercise can be done anytime you sense that your partner is upset and you'd like to know if you are right about the reasons for it. Every couple mind reads every day. This exercise just makes that habit up front and more useful.

To get the feel of how this exercise works, consider how your partner was thinking or feeling about something in your relationship that happened within the last couple of days. Of course, this exercise is most helpful when used in the present tense (while you are in the midst of an experience), but to get the hang of it, you'll bring up something that's already happened—something that you never really processed but made assumptions about (e.g., you think she was upset when you didn't show up on time). Once you have that in mind, complete this sentence:

I think you were _____

_____

_____

Now, ask her how accurate you are in this assumption and note it on the following scale:

Completely Inaccurate   Right on the Money

| 1 | 2 | 3 | 4 | 5 | 6 | 7 | 8 | 9 | 10 |

Again, the point of this simple exercise is to diffuse your natural inclination to "mind read" by making your assumptions known. You'll be amazed how handy this can be in the midst of an intense conversation.

SHARING WITHHOLDS

THIS EXERCISE WILL HELP YOU and your partner keep a clean emotional slate and avoid needless conflicts. We call it "sharing withholds" because it gives you the chance to share thoughts and feelings you may have withheld from each other. It will take about ten to fifteen minutes, and many couples find it helpful to do this exercise on a weekly basis.

Begin by writing two things your partner has done in the last forty-eight hours that you sincerely appreciated but did not tell her. For example, "I appreciate the compliment you gave me as I got out of the car yesterday, and I never did tell you," or "I appreciate the help you gave me in writing my proposal last night, and I don't think you know how much that meant to me."

I appreciate . . .

_____

I appreciate . . .

_____

Next, write one thing your partner has done in the last forty-eight hours that irritated you, but which you did not say anything about. For example, "I didn't like it when you borrowed my umbrella without telling me," or "I didn't like it when you said nothing about the meal I prepared for us last night."

83

Once both of you have written your statements, take turns sharing them. One person shares all three statements one after the other—we recommend sandwiching the negative withhold between the two positives when you share them. Then the other person shares his or her three statements.

And here is an important part of this exercise: The person on the receiving end can say only "thank you" after each statement. That's all. Just "thank you." This rule allows couples to share something that bugs them without fearing a blowup or a defensive reaction. It also allows couples to receive critiques in the context of affirmation.

Here's another important piece to this exercise: Once you've both shared your withholds, neither of you can talk about the negative withhold you just heard for thirty minutes. Why? Because in a half hour's time you will have become more rational and thoughtful. At that point you can then ask your partner questions about it and are far less likely to have an emotional reaction. At that time, too, you may simply be inclined to offer an apology if appropriate. The point is not to stir up a fight where there was none. The point is to clear the "emotional land mines" from your marriage by keeping you current and not allowing painful wounds, even minor ones, to fester.

This exercise can be done weekly as we mentioned. Once you get the hang of it, you don't necessarily need to write your statements down, but it's often helpful. You may also want to agree on a routine time when you can do this exercise each week (e.g., Wednesdays after dinner) so one of you doesn't have to always initiate it. If you put this into practice by making it a weekly habit, we think you'll agree that sharing withholds can save you hundreds of hours of needless bickering.

CREATING A CLEAN SLATE

To PARAPHRASE IVY BAKER PRIEST, the end may also be the beginning—if you start again with a clean slate. So if you are entering marriage for the second time, we want to help you do that through this workbook exercise.

Write a short history of your former relationship by completing the following sentence stems:

1. The things that initially attracted me to my first wife were ...

_____

_____

2. I decided to marry my first wife because ...

_____

_____

3. My first wife contributed to making our marriage work by ...

_____

_____

4. I personally contributed to the relationship's difficulties by ...

_____

_____

5. I still feel angry about . . .

_____

_____

6. I still feel guilty about . . .

_____

_____

7. I still feel sad about . . .

_____

_____

8. A lesson I've learned about marriage that I'll apply in my second marriage is . . .

_____

_____

9. What my first marriage taught me about myself is . . .

_____

_____

Once you have taken the time to seriously contemplate and respond to each of these items, set aside some meaningful time to discuss them with your partner. If she has been married before, you can take turns responding to each of these items.

REMARRIED WITH CHILDREN

So you are about to plunge into a new marriage that comes prepackaged with children. Are you ready? Most people would say you're not fully equipped until you've devised a plan. In this exercise we offer a way to get you started in doing just that.

Below is a list of important pointers for building a successful combined family. Read through the list and rank the top half-dozen items you feel are most important for you. It is important to do this on your own at first without influence from your partner.

___ Start out in our own new place. This will eliminate turf squabbles, alleviate hurt feelings, and allow us to rid ourselves of the ghosts of the past.

___ Ease into the relationships with our children and let them develop gradually. Relationships do not develop on demand. Trust takes time.

___ Develop our own new traditions as a family. These will hasten our sense of belonging and connectedness as we develop familiar routines and special celebrations.

___ Negotiate differences instead of fighting over right and wrong. Whether we let the dog sleep at the foot of the bed or in the garage is not a matter of right or wrong but simply a difference in preference.

___ Maintain a special, planned, one-on-one time that allows our relationship to grow and be nourished in the midst of learning to parent together.

___ Support our children's access to both biological parents. We do not want our children to be caught in the middle, nor do we want them to be emotionally torn apart.

___ Adults in both households will make direct contact with each other to work out residential schedules with input from the children. We will not talk to each other through the children.

___ We understand that much of a child's anger comes from changes and losses they have not chosen. Sharing a parent, a room, or toy with stepsiblings; going to a new school; missing your other parent, friends, and former neighborhood; having unfamiliar food; adjusting to new rules — all make for some guaranteed difficulties that we will work to understand.

___ We will do all we can to learn about the dynamics of stepfamily situations. We will read books, talk to other stepparents, and attend seminars that will sharpen our skills as we work together as a parental team.

___ Biological parents and ex-spouses will strive to be cooperative coparents with one another. We will compartmentalize our anger and hurt so we can cooperate on issues regarding the children's wellbeing. We know that if our conflict continues, the children will suffer.

Once you have ranked your items, compare notes with your partner. Discuss the items each of you checked and explain why. Then use these items to devise a plan for building your combined family together.

Exercise Twenty-Six

YOUR SPIRITUAL JOURNEY

THIS EXERCISE WILL HELP YOU and your partner share your individual pilgrimages. It will take about fifteen to twenty-five minutes.

Part of cultivating spiritual intimacy comes from merging two individual journeys. We are all beginners when it comes to spiritual development, but each of us has come from a different place and traveled a different road to meet where we are today. You may have grown up in a religious home learning Bible verses, going to Sunday school, and studying at a Christian college. Or maybe you never went to church while growing up and are just becoming grounded in your faith. Whatever your story, take a moment to gather your thoughts about your own spiritual quest. Then make a few notes of some of the significant mile markers.

Next, take a moment to complete this brief quiz.

Agree	Disagree	Spouses should . . .
☐	☐	Pray together every day.
☐	☐	Study the Bible together regularly.
☐	☐	Discuss spiritual issues.
☐	☐	Go to the same church.
☐	☐	Agree on theology.
☐	☐	Pay a tithe.
☐	☐	Pray for each other.
☐	☐	Leave each other's spiritual life up to God.
☐	☐	Have the same level of spiritual maturity.
☐	☐	Attend church at least once a week.

Once you have gathered your thoughts and completed the quiz, share your journey with your partner. Discuss what has brought you to where you are today. Also, compare how each of you responded to the quiz. Use it as a springboard to a deeper discussion of how each of you views spiritual matters.

Next, seek to understand how both you and your partner love God. This can be revolutionary for some couples. In his helpful book *Sacred Pathways* (Zondervan, 2002), Gary Thomas describes nine ways we tend to relate to God. Rank the top two or three styles that fit you best. Then try to predict your partner's top pathways before comparing notes.

Me	*My Partner*	
☐	☐	*The Traditionalist* loves God through rituals, sacraments, and symbols throughout the year.
☐	☐	*The Visionary* loves God by dreaming a great dream to accomplish great things.
☐	☐	*The Socialite* loves God best around other people, confiding in them and being accountable to them.
☐	☐	*The Intellectual* seeks God with his or her mind by considering a new theological concept.
☐	☐	*The Caregiver* loves God by being compassionate and loving others even if it means significant sacrifice.
☐	☐	*The Contemplative* seeks to love God in a quiet pursuit of journaling and reflection.
☐	☐	*The Activist* is at war with injustice and loves God by fighting it.
☐	☐	*The Naturalist* feels closest to God in the out-of-doors in the midst of creation.
☐	☐	*The Worshiper* is inspired by joyful celebration and music.

Now, jot down some specific ways these pathways are manifested in your life. If you are a Contemplative, for example, what do you like to do, where do you like to go, and how much time do you like to spend, to be close to God?

_____

_____

_____

Once you and your partner have both noted the top two or three styles that fit you best, spend a few minutes comparing them and discuss what you might learn from each other's pathways.

If you are using the SYMBIS Assessment you will want to also refer to the Dynamics: Spirituality portion of your personalized report. It provides further exploration of how your personalities and desires impact your spiritual journey together.

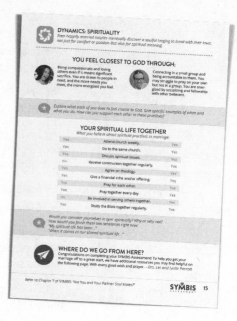

IMPROVING YOUR SERVE

THIS EXERCISE WILL HELP YOU and your partner cultivate a soulful marriage by reaching out to others. It will take about ten to fifteen minutes.

Here are a few of the ways couples have practiced the fine art of serving others:

- Volunteering in a youth group
- Supporting someone's education
- Taking care of a shut-in's lawn
- Welcoming new people to the neighborhood
- Doing short-term relief trips overseas
- Sending helpful books to people

Take a moment to list a few ways that you and your partner might reach out together as a team. Work on your own and be as creative as you can before sharing your thoughts with your partner.

Now compare your list with your partner's. Combine your lists and begin to rank the items in order of what both of you might like to do as a team. Once you have a couple of things that seem like they might fit your joint style, discuss in more detail what they might actually look like.

1. How would the two of you actually live out these forms of service?

_____

_____

_____

2. What do you think reaching out to others might do for your marriage?

_____

_____

_____

STUDY YOUR SPOUSE

THIS EXERCISE WILL HELP YOU understand your partner's unique needs now and in the future. It will take about five to ten minutes *each day*.

No one can play as significant a role in encouraging your partner as you. No one can meet her needs better than you. But to be effective, you must study your partner by paying careful attention to her needs, desires, and aspirations.

This exercise is simply a prayer. It need not involve any sharing or discussion with your partner. It simply asks you to study and pray.

> *God, our Creator, you were there when my partner was formed. You knit her together in her mother's womb. You know her every thought, need, and desire. You are acquainted with all her ways. Enlighten me. Teach me to know this complicated woman you have given me to love.*

Record any of your thoughts or observations below as you consider how you can better understand and study your soul mate. How does your new understanding of your partner change the way you treat her? Here are a few follow-up questions to help you structure your thoughts and review the content of *Saving Your Second Marriage Before It Starts*:

1. What can you keep in mind about her expectations (shaped by the family she came from) that will allow you to have a deeper understanding of her?

_____

_____

_____

_____

2. As you think about her definition of love (what makes her feel loved by you) as well as the three essential ingredients of love (passion, intimacy, and commitment), what are the actions you can intentionally take and observations you can make to express your love to her?

_____

_____

_____

_____

3. When you think about "the habit of happiness" as it relates to her, what can you keep in mind about her internal "self-talk" and what helps her to keep a positive attitude?

_____

_____

_____

_____

4. What kinds of conversations does she most enjoy, and when are you most likely to experience them?

_____

_____

_____

_____

_____

5. As you bridge the gender gap in your marriage, what will serve you well to keep in mind about her as a woman?

_____

_____

_____

_____

_____

6. What issues are most likely to result in frustration and tension for her (what are her hot topics?), and what can you learn to do better to resolve conflicts with her?

_____

_____

_____

_____

_____

7. As you consider her spiritual journey, what can you do to help her carve out a path to God that is meaningful in your marriage?

_____

_____

_____

_____

_____

Study your partner. Listen to her, talk to her. And every day, pray this simple prayer, asking God to help you understand her better.

SESSIONS

*For Group or Couple
Discussion with the
Group Video Series*

INTRODUCTION

STUDYING THIS MATERIAL IN A GROUP with other couples is one of the best ways to make it stick—and have a lot of fun in the process. To that end, we've created this nine-session group discussion guide. Most people feel this is just about the right length for a group series. Though we've created this discussion guide for group or classroom use, it is also adaptable for individual couple's study if you and your partner prefer to go through the questions on your own or are unable to connect with others who are studying the same curriculum.

Before your group meetings, it would be helpful for you to read the assigned chapters associated with the session, but this is not required. Obviously, you are going to get more out of the discussion if you've "done your homework." So if you can make the time to read the chapters, great! If not, don't worry. You can still join in on the discussion (it doesn't rely on having read the chapters), and you don't need to feel an ounce of guilt. The purpose is to enjoy the interaction and to learn from it. You can always read the chapters later, if you wish.

Here's a quick glimpse at what you'll be doing in each group session. We've designed each session to last about an hour, but you can take more or less time as your schedule dictates.

JUST FOR FUN
(4 MINUTES)

Each session begins with a question or activity that is "just for fun"—a kind of icebreaker. These are just to get the wheels turning and to help you connect as you come together as a group.

101

VIDEO NOTES
(15 – 30 MINUTES)

In addition to hearing from Les and Leslie Parrott, each session will include two brief video segments featuring several real-life couples who are exploring these issues just as you are. As you watch the DVD or digital session, feel free to fill in the content points supplied, in addition to jotting down your notes, questions, and reactions in the space provided.

EXPLORING YOUR WORKBOOK EXERCISE
(15 – 20 MINUTES)

Each of the sessions will rely on an exercise from this workbook. You will typically spend time within the group session doing the exercise, then discussing it. While of course it would be helpful to have the exercises completed beforehand, you may do them within your group if you wish. We've selected exercises that will not put anyone on the spot or force anyone to share information they don't want to. Of course, your group may elect to use other exercises from this workbook to discuss if you wish. That's up to you and your group. But we will point you to the exercises in this workbook that we feel are most suitable.

TIME TO DISCUSS
(20 MINUTES)

The list of questions you'll find in this section is designed to spark ideas, reactions, and real-life examples. As you interact, remember that a key ingredient to successful group discussion is vulnerability. This doesn't mean you have to say anything you don't want to. It's just that, typically, the more transparent you are, the more meaningful the experience will be, and the more open others will be as well. Vulnerability begets vulnerability. However, we caution you not to use this time to gripe about your partner in some way. Don't embarrass each other by dragging out dirty laundry you know would upset your partner. You want to be genuine and vulnerable, but not at the expense of your partner's feelings.

Another key ingredient in these discussions is specificity. You'll gain much more out of this time when you use specific examples with each other. So with this in mind, we will remind you to "be specific" every so often.

Finally, if you are a group facilitator, don't feel that you need to follow the order given or even use every question. Let the dynamics of the discussion be your guide.

YOUR SYMBIS ASSESSMENT

If you are using the SYMBIS Assessment, this section will direct you to the pertinent pages of your report and help you explore the personal information on these pages within the context of each video session. While we have placed this section toward the end of the session flow, feel free to move it earlier in your session if you like. (Note: No time allotment has been suggested for this component. If you include an assessment discussion as part of your session and are restricted to an hour of group time, adjust the other time frames accordingly.)

TAKING TIME AS A COUPLE

Finally, we've included suggestions for ways you can take this group experience into your week together as a couple. We encourage you to further discuss and apply the material as a way to connect and grow together. And of course you can also read the book together or individually if you can make the time. Again, no pressure or guilt.

One more thing: Relax. Have fun. And enjoy the opportunity to master life skills that will improve your relationship and help you develop a strong foundation for a marriage that will last a lifetime.

Session One

ARE YOU READY TO GET MARRIED AGAIN?

WHETHER IT'S ONE PARTNER or both who are entering a second marriage, being fully prepared for the unique challenges remarriage presents is essential. This session will help you explore critical marriage issues that you'll want to address—so you are both ready for a relationship that lasts a lifetime.

JUST FOR FUN
(4 MINUTES)

Describe your first impression of each other. What was that first encounter like, and how has your first impression changed from then to now? How has it remained the same?

VIDEO SEGMENT #1 NOTES
(7 MINUTES)

- Reasons to _____ remarry

- The most important reason to get married again is
_____.

EXPLORING YOUR WORKBOOK EXERCISE
(15 MINUTES)

Within your group, complete exercise 2 in your workbook (page 18). Discuss your responses with the group. Remember, there's no need to disclose anything you feel is too personal or private, but share what you learned about yourself and your relationship as a result of completing this exercise.

VIDEO SEGMENT #2 NOTES
(7 MINUTES)

- _____ readiness

- _____ readiness

- Your marriage can only be as _____ as the two of you.

TIME TO DISCUSS
(20 MINUTES)

1. What have you heard about remarriage (from friends, family, media, and so on)?

_____

_____

_____

_____

_____

2. In the video session you just watched, what comments from couples in this session do you most resonate with and why?

_____

_____

_____

_____

_____

3. What does "relational readiness for remarriage" mean to you? How do you know when the relationship is in a good place to move into remarriage?

_____

_____

_____

_____

_____

4. In your opinion, what is likely to be a unique challenge you might face as a couple involved in a remarriage?

_____

_____

_____

_____

_____

YOUR SYMBIS ASSESSMENT

If you are using the SYMBIS Assessment, review the Context: Remarriage section (page 7A) of your report. Explore your individual motivations to remarry; how are they similar and different? Of course, you will only have information on this page if you are marrying again. If it's a first marriage for one of you, this will still be a helpful conversation. Do the same thing for the portion about your remarriage readiness.

TAKING TIME AS A COUPLE

To further explore whether you are ready for remarriage, spend some time this week as a couple reading chapter 1 and completing exercise 1 in the workbook. If you have time, also discuss the reflection questions with your partner.

Session Two

HAVE YOU FACED THE MYTHS OF MARRIAGE WITH HONESTY?

What you believe about marriage will become the fuel for your behavior in marriage. For this reason, exploring the myths of marriage is essential.

JUST FOR FUN
(4 MINUTES)

Whether you are doing this as an individual couple or as a small group of couples, take a moment to name one of the most romantic movies you've ever seen. It could be *The Notebook*, *The Fault in Our Stars*, *Sleepless in Seattle*, *Casablanca*, *Titanic*, *Father of the Bride*, *When Harry Met Sally*, or any of the hundreds of other romantic stories. What makes this movie so romantic to you? Do you see yourself in it? From your perspective, what's the primary message of the movie? If you don't like this line of questioning, name a romantic movie that you didn't like. Why?

VIDEO SEGMENT #1 NOTES
(17 MINUTES)

- Your beliefs are the fuel for your behavior.

- Myth #1: We expect the _____ from marriage.

- _____ Rules

- _____ Roles

EXPLORING YOUR WORKBOOK EXERCISE
(20 MINUTES)

Within your small group, take time to complete exercise 4 in your workbook (page 24). This exercise explores making conscious your understanding of the roles both you and your partner have in a marriage. If you are comfortable, share with the group: What insights did you have while doing this exercise? How have your families of origin influenced your understanding of roles? What items did you have to renegotiate?

VIDEO SEGMENT #2 NOTES
(12 MINUTES)

- Myth #2: Everything _____ will get better.

- Myth #3: Everything _____ will disappear.

- Myth #4: Adjustment to married life occurs more _____ in remarriage.

- Myth #5: My spouse will make me _____.

- If you try to build intimacy with another person before getting whole on your own, all your relationships become an attempt to complete yourself.

- A-Frame Relationship = overly _____

- H-Frame Relationship = overly _____

- M-Frame Relationship = _____

TIME TO DISCUSS
(20 MINUTES)

1. Which ideas expressed in the video were new to you?

_____

_____

_____

_____

2. Which concept talked about in today's session can you apply to your relationship?

_____

_____

3. In what areas of your life is your relationship operating as an **A**, **H**, or **M**?

_____

_____

_____

_____

4. What other myths do couples bring to the marriage relationship?

_____

_____

_____

YOUR SYMBIS ASSESSMENT

If you are using the SYMBIS Assessment, review the Context section of your report (pages 5–7). What myths of marriage might you debunk as a result of seeing this personal information on these pages? For example, "we are going to do everything together," is a common misbelief. Page 7 of your report will make this plain.

TAKING TIME AS A COUPLE

To further explore marital myths you may have believed, spend some time this week as a couple reading chapter 2 and completing exercises 1, 3, 5, 6, and 7 in the workbook. If you have time, also discuss the reflection questions with your partner.

Session Three

CAN YOU IDENTIFY YOUR LOVE STYLE?

Do you have a crystal clear concept of love? And do you see it the same way as your partner? This session will ensure that you get on the same page as you write your love story together.

JUST FOR FUN
(4 MINUTES)

Whether you are doing this as an individual couple or as a small group of couples, take a moment to answer these questions together: If you were designing a recipe for the perfect romantic day, and money wasn't an object, what would go into it and why? What would you do together to cultivate romance for twenty-four hours with an unlimited budget? As you reflect on this daydream, consider how romance relates to love. In other words, what percentage of married love do you think involves romance?

VIDEO SEGMENT #1 NOTES
(13 MINUTES)

- Passion is the _____ component of love.

- Intimacy is the _____ component of love.

- Commitment is the _____ component of love.

EXPLORING YOUR WORKBOOK EXERCISE
(15 MINUTES)

Within your small group, take time to complete exercise 8 in your workbook (page 35). This exercise should help you define love in your own terms and compare your definition with your partner's. What qualities of love were most important to you? To your partner? Discuss with the group how your definition of love compared to your partner's.

VIDEO SEGMENT #2 NOTES
(17 MINUTES)

• How to cultivate passion (for women): _____

• How to cultivate intimacy (for men): _____

• How to cultivate commitment (for both men and women):

_____

TIME TO DISCUSS
(20 MINUTES)

1. Which idea presented in today's session did you find most interesting? Why?

_____

_____

_____

_____

2. In your love life right now, which component of love seems most powerful: passion, intimacy, or commitment? Why?

_____

_____

_____

_____

3. In what ways can you nurture each component of love: passion, intimacy, and commitment?

_____

_____

_____

_____

4. Why is it important to remember that love is constantly changing and growing?

_____

_____

_____

_____

YOUR SYMBIS ASSESSMENT

If you are using the SYMBIS Assessment, review the Dynamics: Love section (page 10) of your report. How do your unique personalities view love in practical terms? Explore your two unique definitions of love and the top three ingredients that matter most to each of you.

TAKING TIME AS A COUPLE

In order to better understand your love style, spend some time this week as a couple reading chapter 3 and completing exercises 10 and 11 in the workbook. If you have time, also discuss the reflection questions with your partner.

Session Four

HAVE YOU DEVELOPED THE HABIT OF HAPPINESS?

This habit can make or break a marriage. And it's important to remember that it has little to do with your partner and everything to do with you. In other words, an upbeat attitude is highly contagious.

JUST FOR FUN
(4 MINUTES)

Whether you are doing this as an individual couple or as a small group of couples, take a moment to answer these questions together: Consider a time when you had "one of those days"—a time when nothing seemed to go as planned. Looking back on it, can you find any humor in it? If your experience was written into a sitcom, what would the name of the show be called and why? Now, think about how you typically respond when unexpected circumstances interrupt your plans. Anything you'd like to change about your attitude in these times?

VIDEO SEGMENT #1 NOTES
(10 MINUTES)

- The one habit that can make or break your relationship is the

  capacity to adjust to things _____ your control.

- The most important quality of a marriageable person is the habit of _____.

EXPLORING YOUR WORKBOOK EXERCISE
(15 MINUTES)

Within your group, complete exercise 12 in your workbook (page 49). Share with others how you see your attitude shaping the moods of your marriage. What types of things affect your mood? What negative self-talk have you used, and how can you help your partner avoid negative self-talk that she might use?

VIDEO SEGMENT #2 NOTES
(9 MINUTES)

- The three toxins that can seep into a marriage relationship:

_____, _____,

_____

TIME TO DISCUSS
(20 MINUTES)

1. What struck you most about today's session?

_____

_____

_____

_____

_____

2. When are you most likely to blame your partner?

3. Do you think the most important quality of a marriageable person is the habit of happiness? Why or why not?

4. What keeps you from *choosing* to be happy?

YOUR SYMBIS ASSESSMENT

If you are using the SYMBIS Assessment, review the Dynamics: Attitude section (page 11) of your report. How would each of you describe your abilities to adjust to things beyond your control? In other words, how adaptable and resilient do you see yourselves being when faced with a challenge?

TAKING TIME AS A COUPLE

To further explore how your attitudes can affect your marriage, spend some time this week as a couple reading chapter 4 and completing exercises 13 and 14 in the workbook. If you have time, also discuss the reflection questions with your partner.

Session Five

CAN YOU SAY WHAT YOU MEAN AND UNDERSTAND WHAT YOU HEAR?

Communication is the lifeline of every marriage.
But too often the lines of communication between
couples get crossed. Rest assured that this session will
help you speak each other's language fluently.

JUST FOR FUN
(4 MINUTES)

If you are doing this as a small group of couples, take a moment to play the "whisper" game. One of you begins by whispering something (at least three sentences long)—it can be about anything (what you had for lunch, what you like to do on vacation, your idea of a dream wedding)—and the task is to convey the message around the entire group. You can't ask a person to repeat the message. You simply have to whisper to the next person what you heard. You'll be surprised by how the message ends up. If you are doing this session as an individual couple, talk about a time when you encountered a major miscommunication. What happened?

VIDEO SEGMENT #1 NOTES
(12 MINUTES)

- Men _____ talk.

- Women _____ talk.

- Communication Basics

- Skill #1: _____ content.

EXPLORING YOUR WORKBOOK EXERCISE
(15 MINUTES)

Within your small group, complete exercise 15 in your workbook (page 57). Compare your score with your partner's and discuss how well each of you is communicating. If you are comfortable, share with your group areas in which you can improve your communication.

VIDEO SEGMENT #2 NOTES
(7 MINUTES)

- Communication Basics

- Skill #2: _____ feeling.

- Without being genuine, the best communication techniques in the world will fall flat.

TIME TO DISCUSS
(20 MINUTES)

1. Which ideas presented in today's session were new to you?

_____

_____

_____

_____

_____

2. Which concept presented in this session seems most difficult for you to put into practice?

_____

_____

_____

_____

_____

3. Empathy involves using your head _and_ your heart. Which do you tend to use more — your head or your heart? How can you begin to cultivate using both in your interactions with your partner?

_____

_____

_____

_____

_____

4. When do you feel most understood? When do you feel least understood? In what ways can you better communicate your own feelings about being understood?

_____

_____

_____

_____

_____

YOUR SYMBIS ASSESSMENT

If you are using the SYMBIS Assessment, review the Dynamics: Communication section (page 12) of your report. How would each of you describe your personal "talk styles" (which descriptors do you resonate with most)? From the list on this page, what are the two most important things that your partner needs to know about communicating with you? What is one practical thing you each will do to improve your communication skills?

TAKING TIME AS A COUPLE

To learn more about successful communication in your marriage, spend some time this week as a couple reading chapter 5 and completing exercises 16 and 17 in the workbook. If you have time, also discuss the reflection questions with your partner.

Session Six

HAVE YOU BRIDGED THE GENDER GAP?

Everybody knows that men and women are different. But what most newlywed couples don't realize, until they cross the proverbial threshold, is just how pronounced that difference is. This session will help make that transition much easier.

JUST FOR FUN
(10 MINUTES)

If you are studying this curriculum with other couples, divide into two groups: men in one group and women in another. In each group, appoint a facilitator and a secretary. Answer the question, "What do you want the other gender to know about your gender?" What insights do you gain from hearing what the other group has to say? If you and your partner are completing this on your own, discuss the same question with each other.

VIDEO SEGMENT #1 NOTES
(11 MINUTES)

- How men and women solve problems:

- Men want to _____ it.

- Women want to _____ it.

EXPLORING YOUR WORKBOOK EXERCISE
(20 MINUTES)

Within your group, complete exercise 19 in your workbook (page 67). This exercise should help you communicate your deepest needs to your partner. Share with the group the needs that were most important to you. How did these needs compare with those of your partner? How do you see your needs changing as you grow in your marriage?

VIDEO SEGMENT #2 NOTES
(10 MINUTES)

- Men need _____ activity.

- Women need to be _____.

TIME TO DISCUSS
(15 MINUTES)

1. What ideas did you hear today that were new to you?

_____

_____

_____

_____

_____

2. What general gender differences have you experienced in your relationship?

_____

_____

_____

_____

_____

3. How can these gender differences cause conflict in your marriage?

_____

_____

_____

_____

_____

4. What steps can you take to celebrate the differences you both bring to your marriage?

_____

_____

_____

_____

_____

YOUR SYMBIS ASSESSMENT

If you are using the SYMBIS Assessment, review the Dynamics: Gender section (page 13) of your report. How do you feel about the statements describing what your partner needs from you? What's one practical way that each of you can meet this particular need— especially once you are married? Also, note your top two needs and discuss why they are important to each of you.

TAKING TIME AS A COUPLE

To further explore how gender differences affect your marriage, spend some time this week as a couple reading chapter 6 and completing exercise 18 in the workbook. If you have time, also discuss the reflection questions with your partner.

Session Seven

DO YOU KNOW HOW TO FIGHT A GOOD FIGHT?

Conflict is inevitable. No matter how "in love" a couple is, friction eventually emerges. But the savvy couple knows how to use this conflict to their advantage. This session will show you how.

JUST FOR FUN
(4 MINUTES)

Sometimes people fight about the silliest things—like an insignificant detail in a story they are telling, how someone is driving the car, etc. What's the craziest conflict you have ever heard of and why? Also, have you ever encountered a conflict because you were convinced you were right about something and it turned out you weren't? If so, are you willing to share it?

VIDEO SEGMENT #1 NOTES
(18 MINUTES)

- Negative feelings that get buried have a high rate of resurrection.

EXPLORING YOUR WORKBOOK EXERCISE
(15 MINUTES)

Within your group, complete exercise 23 in your workbook (page 83). The skills learned from this exercise should help you and your partner avoid needless conflicts by remaining emotionally open with one another. If you are comfortable, share with the group how you felt when sharing withholds with your partner.

VIDEO SEGMENT #2 NOTES
(14 MINUTES)

• What to avoid in conflict: _____ ,

_____ , _____ ,

_____

• XYZ Formula: In situation X, when you do Y, I feel Z.

• A great way to turn a _____

into a _____

TIME TO DISCUSS
(20 MINUTES)

1. What causes the biggest conflicts in your relationship?

_____

_____

_____

_____

_____

2. How do you usually handle conflict?

_____

_____

_____

_____

_____

3. As you were growing up, how did your family typically handle conflict? What habits have you taken with you into your adult life?

_____

_____

_____

_____

_____

4. What "conflict habits" have you brought to your new relationship?

_____

_____

_____

_____

_____

YOUR SYMBIS ASSESSMENT

If you are using the SYMBIS Assessment, review the Dynamics: Conflict section (page 14) of your report. What statements within each of your individual "fight types" do you resonate with most? Which of your "personal conflict challenges" do you believe will be the most difficult and why? As you review your "hot topics" together, explore practical ways to alleviate the tension from the top two or three.

TAKING TIME AS A COUPLE

To further explore how to handle conflict in your marriage, spend some time this week as a couple reading chapter 7 and completing exercises 21 and 22 in the workbook. If you have time, also discuss the reflection questions with your partner.

Session Eight

DO YOU KNOW HOW TO BLEND A FAMILY?

IF YOU ARE MARRYING for the second time, you already know there are special challenges that are unique to your situation—especially if you are blending a family. This session is specifically for you.

JUST FOR FUN
(4 MINUTES)

Perhaps the modern-day iconic image of a second marriage situation is found in the 1970s sitcom The Brady Bunch. If you've seen the show, most likely in reruns, take a moment to talk about it. What are some of the memories you have from watching this program? And what, if anything, did the show have to say about a second marriage where kids are involved? If you haven't seen the show, talk about how the media generally portrays blended families.

VIDEO SEGMENT #1 NOTES
(9 MINUTES)

- Takes a minimum of _____ years

- Completing your own _____ business

- Being _____ to your ex

- Be the _____ disciplinarian.

- _____ for the nonbiological spouse

- You can't _____ the missing parent.

- Take a _____ course.

- Give _____ to the children and biological parent.

EXPLORING YOUR WORKBOOK EXERCISE
(20 MINUTES)

Within your group, take time to complete exercise 25 in your workbook (page 87). This exercise will help you determine what is most important for you in building a successful combined family. Discuss your responses with your partner before sharing with the group. Remember, there's no need to disclose anything you feel is too personal or private.

VIDEO SEGMENT #2 NOTES
(6 MINUTES)

- Make the new _____ paramount.

- Begin _____ family traditions.

- Respect _____ family traditions.

- Hold a _____ meeting.

- Protect everyone's _____ space.

- Don't _____ into having your own child together.

TIME TO DISCUSS
(20 MINUTES)

1. If you are the biological parent, what is one specific thing you can do to improve the blending process? Is there anything about your personal situation that will make blending your family more difficult?

_____

_____

_____

_____

2. Discipline is a big issue in blended families. If you are the biological parent, how can you take some concrete steps to be the primary disciplinarian?

_____

_____

_____

_____

3. If you are a stepparent, it can sometimes be tough to give your spouse time alone with his or her biological children. What can you do to feel good about this and ensure that it happens?

_____

_____

_____

4. Consider building new family traditions and activities into your blended family. What might they be? How can you respect the old traditions while building new ones?

YOUR SYMBIS ASSESSMENT

If you are using the SYMBIS Assessment, review the Context: Blending a Family section (page 7A) of your report. If one or both of you are bringing a child into the relationship, explore the information related to how the two of you will blend a family. Which of the statements is most important to you and why.

TAKING TIME AS A COUPLE

To further explore the topic of blending a family, take time this week as a couple reading chapter 8 and completing exercise 24 in the workbook.

Session Nine

ARE YOU AND YOUR PARTNER SOUL MATES?

*You can do everything right in marriage and still wake up one
morning and wonder, "Is this it?" You will continually be looking
for depth and meaning in your relationship until you explore
your spiritual nature — how the two of you walk together
with God. This session will show you how to do just that.*

JUST FOR FUN
(4 MINUTES)

Research shows that married couples who pray together enjoy a
better sex life. What do you think of that? Why do you think this is
so? And what does it say to you about the spiritual aspect of a married couple's life together?

VIDEO SEGMENT #1 NOTES
(7 MINUTES)

- On a scale of 1 to 10, most churchgoing couples rate the
  importance of spiritual intimacy as a 9 or 10, yet rate the
  level of satisfaction with their spiritual intimacy as a 2 or 3.
- Couples who pray together report higher satisfaction with
  their sex lives.

EXPLORING YOUR WORKBOOK EXERCISE
(15 MINUTES)

Within your group, complete exercise 27 in your workbook (page 93). This exercise explores reaching out to others as a way to strengthen your marriage. What are some activities you and your partner came up with to serve others? How do you think this service will impact your marriage?

VIDEO SEGMENT #2 NOTES
(8 MINUTES)

- When it comes to cultivating spiritual intimacy together, every couple has their own unique style.

TIME TO DISCUSS
(20 MINUTES)

1. On a scale of 1 to 10, how important is spiritual intimacy in your marriage? Explain your answer.

_____

_____

_____

_____

2. On that same scale of 1 to 10, how satisfied are you with your current level of spiritual intimacy? Explain your answer.

_____

_____

_____

_____

_____

3. What are you presently doing in the area of shared service?

_____

_____

_____

_____

_____

4. What is one thing you can do as a couple to strengthen the spiritual aspect of your relationship?

_____

_____

_____

_____

_____

YOUR SYMBIS ASSESSMENT

If you are using the SYMBIS Assessment, review the Dynamics: Spirituality section (page 15) of your report. How would you elaborate on the descriptions at the top of this page? What do you do in practical terms to draw closer to God? Would you expect your partner to do the same? Why or why not? Review "your spiritual life together." What practices do you agree with most? What practices do you two need to discuss in greater depth and why?

TAKING TIME AS A COUPLE

To further explore the spiritual nature of your marriage, spend some time this week as a couple reading chapter 9 and completing exercises 26 and 28 in the workbook. If you have time, also discuss the reflection questions with your partner.

GIVE THE VERY BEST TO

You won't find a more personalized and powerful pre-marriage assessment than SYMBIS.

"The SYMBIS Assessment rocks! We learned so much about our relationship and feel incredibly confident about our future together."
-Toni & Chris

Get your personalized 15-page report!

YOUR RELATIONSHIP

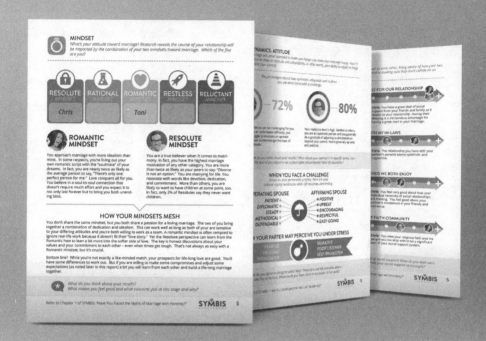

EVERYTHING YOU NEED TO KNOW ABOUT:

- **Your Personalities** – *discover your strengths*
- **Your Love Life** – *cultivate deeper passion*
- **Your Fight Types** – *discover your "hot topics"*
- **Your Talk Styles** – *crack your intimacy codes*
- **Your Money Methods** – *kick financial woes to the curb*

*And so much more. **Plus**, it works seamlessly with the SYMBIS book and his/her workbooks.*

Take the assessment: **SYMBISassessment.com**

DVD

his & hers
workbooks

WORKBOOK FOR MEN
Includes 24 Self-Tests and Group Discussion Guide

WORKBOOK FOR WOMEN
Includes 24 Self-Tests and Group Discussion Guide

SAVING YOUR
MARRIAGE
BEFORE IT STARTS
Seven Questions to Ask Before - and After - You Marry

SAVING YOUR
MARRIAGE
BEFORE IT STARTS
Seven Questions to Ask Before - and After - You Marry

SAVING YOUR
MARRIAGE
BEFORE IT STARTS
Seven Questions to Ask
Before - and After - You Marry
SEVEN SESSIONS

Drs. Les & Leslie Parrott
#1 New York Times Bestselling Authors

Drs. Les & Leslie Parrott
#1 New York Times Bestselling Authors

Drs. Les & Leslie Parrott

SYMBIS

SYMBIS

ZONDERVAN

NEWLY EXPANDED EDITION

NEWLY EXPANDED EDITION

Bible
studies

WORKBOOK FOR WOMEN
Includes 24 Self-Tests and Group Discussion Guide

WORKBOOK FOR MEN
Includes 24 Self-Tests and Group Discussion Guide

SAVING YOUR
SECOND
MARRIAGE
BEFORE IT STARTS
Nine Questions to Ask Before - and After - You Remarry

SAVING YOUR
SECOND
MARRIAGE
BEFORE IT STARTS
Nine Questions to Ask Before - and After - You Remarry

SAVING YOUR
SECOND
MARRIAGE
BEFORE IT STARTS
Nine Questions to Ask
Before - and After - You Marry
NINE SESSIONS

Drs. Les & Leslie Parrott
#1 New York Times Bestselling Authors

Drs. Les & Leslie Parrott

ZONDERVAN

SYMBIS

NEWLY EXPANDED EDITION

remarriage
DVD

remarriage
workbooks